T0117785

THE
UNICORN'S
SHADOW

ETHAN
MOLLICK THE
UNICORN'S
SHADOW

COMBATING THE
DANGEROUS MYTHS
THAT HOLD BACK STARTUPS,
FOUNDERS, AND INVESTORS

WHARTON
SCHOOL
PRESS

© 2020 by Ethan Mollick

Published by Wharton School Press
The Wharton School
University of Pennsylvania
3620 Locust Walk
300 Steinberg Hall-Dietrich Hall
Philadelphia, PA 19104
Email: whartonschoolpress@wharton.upenn.edu
Website: wsp.wharton.upenn.edu

All rights reserved. No part of this book may be reproduced, in any form or by any means, without written permission of the publisher. Company and product names mentioned herein are the trademarks or registered trademarks of their respective owners.

Ebook ISBN: 978-1-61363-097-6
Paperback ISBN: 978-1-61363-096–9
Hardcover ISBN: 978-1-61363-095-2

For Lilach, for being the best editor and partner in everything

For Daniel and Miranda, because they are awesome

Contents

Introduction

L et me tell you a story about a startup. . . .

The undergraduate founder coded at night in his dorm room at Stanford, creating a new kind of social network. Though he was awkward and had few friends, he knew he needed a cofounder. His sister wanted to partner with him, but he knew better than to work with her. Instead he found a charismatic guy at a party who was enrolled in the same classes as him and, even better, was an ETSP in the Myers-Briggs test—the entrepreneur personality type! They decided to become partners on the spot, and, realizing that planning meant nothing in the fast-changing world of startups, they got to work immediately. Even though they were new at this, and the idea was outside the mainstream, they found a perceptive angel investor who had identified many hits and decided to back them. The founder and his partner soon found themselves running a giant global company, one that would change how we all communicate. . . .

Seems pretty vivid, right? You can fill in the details: the garage (or maybe run-down frat house) filled with workaholic young programmers in the early days of the company, the founder wearing an ill-fitting suit to the investor meeting while his partner does the talking, and even the giant all-night parties as the company takes off. This is such a vivid picture because it matches a sort of universal startup monomyth—one that looms over aspiring entrepreneurs. Folklorist Joseph Campbell used the term *monomyth* to refer to the fact that the myths of different cultures share common elements that you can see in any story of heroes, from Hercules to Luke Skywalker. The startup monomyth works the same way—elements of the story above contain echoes of famous startups like Facebook, Google, Microsoft, Twitter, and Apple, and some infamous ones, like Theranos.

These are the legendary unicorns, with valuations of over $1 billion, that inform so much of the popular imagination about startups. And because these unicorns are the public-facing rock stars of the entrepreneurial world, they have an outsized influence over the imagination of founders and the public at large. They cast a shadow in their own shape over everything else. People want to be like these companies. They find themselves emulating these organizations.

But they don't have to—and they probably shouldn't. I wrote this book to tell you why and to reveal how the stories we carry around about startups hold back founders, investors, and entrepreneurship in general.

I can do this because the study of entrepreneurship has been in the midst of an empirical revolution. New data, better research methods, and a host of smart scholars have been overturning the conventional wisdom behind what successful founders look like, how they succeed, and how the startup ecosystem works. In this book, we will look at the latest evidence on how to build successful startups and the way in which startups can use a scientific approach to gather their own data to increase their chances of success. At the Wharton School, the business school of the University of Pennsylvania, we call this method Evidence-Based Entrepreneurship.

It's tempting to say that Evidence-Based Entrepreneurship has been the sole key to the tremendous success of Penn grads in the world of startups. In 2018, for example, University of Pennsylvania graduates raised more venture capital money than was raised in all of France and Germany put together. But this fact alone should give you pause. My students are terrific, but are they really worthy of more investment than everyone in two of the world's largest and most innovative economies? This disproportionate investment illustrates that the myths of entrepreneurship have greatly distorted the way that opportunities and talents are supported to the benefit of my students, but to the detriment of many others, a topic we will come back to later in this book.

We'll also explore where the best startup ideas come from, the best ways to go about funding your enterprise, and how to effectively pitch your idea to investors. I have lived and worked in the world of startups throughout my entire career. I have cofounded successful internet companies and nonprofit organizations and have sat on the advisory boards of even more. Startups are also the subject of my academic research and the classes that I teach. But the evidence I will present to you in this book goes beyond my work to include fascinating research done by my colleagues at Wharton and other institutions around the world. And I provide additional information on the book's website, including useful tools, files, and links, which you can access at *www.unicorns-shadow.com*.

Just as I will encourage you to be skeptical of the received wisdom around startup success, I also would encourage you to be skeptical of the evidence that I present and the ways in which I interpret that evidence. This book combines research from nearly 150 academic papers and manuscripts, and each paper has its own strengths and limitations. If there is a particular fact or piece of information that you want to challenge or understand further, I would urge you to look at the cited paper. I would only ask that you recognize that any errors or misinterpretations are my own, rather than the colleagues and peers that I cite. Even with these caveats, I think there is value in looking at the collected evidence around what makes founders successful. If nothing else, it provides a useful counterpoint to the ubiquitous stories of the unicorns. We are still in the early days of understanding startups, and we continue to learn and build out the real, messy, complicated, and sometimes counterintuitive story behind the myths.

Chapter 1

Founders
*Zuckerberg's Shade and the
Specter of Gates*

A specter is haunting potential entrepreneurs—the specter of the ideal founder. Everyone can name at least a few successful entrepreneurs. Think SpaceX founder and Tesla cofounder Elon Musk. Or Microsoft cofounder Bill Gates. Or Facebook cofounder Mark Zuckerberg. So, when people consider starting a company, they often compare themselves to the successful founders they know. Chances are, they will find they don't fit the part: They are too old, the wrong gender, not technical, too caring, not educated enough, or any one of a thousand other points of differentiation.

This has had a dampening effect on entrepreneurship overall. The evidence shows that potential founders are discouraged from starting companies because they don't think of themselves as "looking like" the popular view of an entrepreneur. Research has shown that women, in particular, may be discouraged for this reason.[1] The latest evidence, however, shows that the most successful founders look very different from Zuckerberg or Gates. In fact, following the examples of these canonical entrepreneurs is *more* likely to end in failure than other approaches.

Younger Founders, Older Founders

In my conversations with venture capitalists, it is clear that they often think of founding as a young person's game. For example, Paul Graham, the founder of startup accelerator Y Combinator, said in

2014 that "the cutoff in investors' heads is 32. After 32, they start to be a little skeptical."[2] Entrepreneurs compete to be on Forbes's "30 Under 30" list, but there is no equivalent hype for a "40 Over 40" list. Why do so many people expect founders to be so young?

This expectation seems to come from two different beliefs. The first is that younger founders are more in touch with new markets and quicker to catch on to new ideas. Zuckerberg, when he was still in his 20s himself, told a Stanford audience that "young people are just smarter." The second belief is that people expect founders to work brutal hours as part of their success. For example, a venture capitalist (VC)* once told me that they would call the offices of founders at one in the morning to see if they were working before making an investment decision. One of these beliefs is mostly wrong, and the other is completely incorrect.

It is true that younger founders might be closer to consumer trends and better at marketing to younger (and perhaps faster-adopting) age groups. Young entrepreneurs are also less likely to be trapped in the belief systems that may make older founders believe something is impossible, creating opportunities for real break-throughs.[3] So, for particular kinds of companies, youth may indeed be an advantage, but that does not apply more broadly.

On the other hand, the idea that grinding away at startups all day (and night) is the key to success has less basis in reality. In fact, a lot of recent research has shown how critical it is for founders to get a good night's sleep and downtime away from work to succeed. Entrepreneurs who go home, recover, and sleep are more creative, inspired, and positive than those who work too hard and don't get enough rest.[4] Although many entrepreneurs experience "crunch time" where they must work extreme hours to meet a deadline, research shows that startups perform much better if this is the exception rather than the rule. Venture capitalists should view a founder with a life separate from work as a positive!

---

* The abbreviation VC can be used to mean both venture capitalists and the venture capital they provide.

The issues of innovativeness and hours worked are only two of the lenses by which a founder might be judged, and they are far from the most important. Though we often praise novice entrepreneurs out to disrupt industries, a substantial amount of evidence suggests that the resources available to founders, including money, contacts, and experience, are big factors in determining how likely it is that a given entrepreneur will succeed. Older founders are more likely to understand an industry and have the social and financial capital, as well as vital contacts, needed to start something that is likely to succeed.

So what's the truth? Research by fellow Wharton professor J. Daniel Kim, working with Pierre Azoulay, Benjamin Jones, and Javier Miranda, has some surprising conclusions. Using US Census data, they studied *every founder in the United States*. The average age of a founder is 42, and that number remains about the same for founders starting companies in hot areas like technology. What about fast-growth companies, the kind that Zuckerberg and Gates founded? In that case, the most successful founders are ages 45 to 59!

Though young founders get more attention, older founders are more common than one might think. Consider entrepreneurs like Reed Hastings, who founded Netflix at 37; Arianna Huffington, who started HuffPost at 55; and classic founders like William Durant, who started General Motors at 47.

The Myth of "It"

Some investors look for particular attitudes or traits in the founders they are thinking of backing. The well-known venture capitalist Chris Sacca has said that "the one thing that sets apart the greatest founders is the feeling of inevitability of their success; they just know it's going to work out."[5]

That sentiment underscores the belief that there is a common personality type for founders. There seems to be some debate about what this type is (the nerdy, self-confident extrovert or the nerdy, self-confident introvert?), but the consensus is that *it* definitely matters, and that experienced investors can tell whether you have *it*. Some organizations, like the group behind the infamous (and bogus) Myers-Briggs test, even argue that you can test personality type to see whether someone will be a successful founder.

But it just isn't true.

For decades, scholars have been exploring the link between founder personality and entrepreneurial outcomes, across hundreds of studies.[6] Though some studies have found provisional connections between startup success and personality, the impact is rather small and requires a match between personality and the stage, nature, and approach of the business in question. There is some indication that successful entrepreneurs may want to have more control over their lives than other people, and that they believe in their abilities more than others as well, but the impact of these factors is not particularly large. This doesn't mean that personality has no impact on startups, but it does mean that there is no simple approach to asking what type of person would be best as a founder. And that means that anyone who judges that you won't be a successful entrepreneur because you don't have *it* is likely wrong.

There is an important caveat to this information, however. Although we can't predict what personalities will succeed at entrepreneurship, it is possible to predict who will try to start a company. One of the biggest factors is overconfidence. Entrepreneurship is a lot like trying to make it as a musician or writer. Many people try because they want to make it big, but few achieve stardom. Since entrepreneurship is risky, people who are attracted to it are often those who think (rightly or wrongly) that they are better than everyone else. Overconfidence has no impact on success, but it does mean that many more overconfident people will try to start companies than more modest people. Other psychological factors in the Big Five Personality Test, such as conscientiousness and openness to experience, also seem to predict the likelihood that someone will try to be a founder. But these factors don't explain who will actually succeed.

Is It Dangerous to Go Alone?

If you talk to venture capitalists, you will hear a lot about "founding teams." In fact, the idea that startups require groups of cofounders is deeply ingrained in the myth of the entrepreneur—think of Steve Jobs and Steve Wozniak at Apple or Hewlett and Packard at, well, Hewlett-Packard. The belief in the need for founding teams is so strong that Y Combinator founder Graham listed it as the first of "18 Mistakes that Kill Startups."[7] Graham's prestigious accelerator, Y Combinator, turned away Drew Houston, the founder of Dropbox, telling him that it would not accept the company into its program unless Houston found a cofounder. Houston turned to a friend of a friend, Arash Ferdowsi, whom he had never met. He convinced Ferdowsi over two hours to drop out of MIT and launch the company with him.[8] Dropbox went on to be a massive success, but this could have been a horror story. Is it really necessary to convince a complete stranger to found a company with you in order to succeed? Why is it so important to have cofounders?

My colleague Jason Greenberg, a professor at New York University's Stern School of Business, and I decided to look at the evidence behind this deeply held myth and found very little to support it. A few older studies suggested that founding teams might outperform individuals, but this was mostly a taken-for-granted assumption.[9] We decided to look into the issue in more detail.

We began by using data drawn from a detailed survey of thousands of companies that launched on Kickstarter. We found that the sample was fairly evenly divided between solo founders, groups of two, and teams of three or more. When we analyzed the data, we found something surprising—the odds of running an ongoing for-profit venture were more than twice as high for the solo founders as for the teams! Startups run by solo founders were actually doing better than cofounded companies.

Reflection helps make sense of this finding. If you have ever seen the movie *The Social Network*, you know that Eduardo Saverin (played by Andrew Garfield) was a cofounder of Facebook, along with

Zuckerberg. They worked together to launch Facebook and invested their own money. Conflict quickly broke out between the two, and Eduardo was eventually forced out of his own company, which he memorably sued. In this case, Facebook was too far along to be stopped by founder conflict, but this story is incredibly common. In a survey, venture capitalists suggested that 65% of the reason that startups fail is because of issues with the senior management team, while only 35% was due to everything else, from products to marketing to functional management.[10] Having cofounders can help share the workload and provide psychological support, but it can also cause conflict.

That doesn't mean that you should definitely found a company alone. There is still relatively little research in this area, and many funders still expect to see cofounder teams. That means that even if founding alone is preferred, it won't help you much if every venture capitalist and angel investor expects you to have a cofounder. But it does suggest that founding alone is an option, especially when your only option is to found with a stranger.

Another research paper that Greenberg and I have written looks at the relationships between founders, using a combination of the crowdfunding data from the previous study and new data from a survey of US founders across many industries. We discovered that founding with a stranger is generally disastrous, with the highest failure rate, even though it worked out for Dropbox. Though this makes sense, a second finding was more surprising: Starting companies with friends with whom you haven't worked is almost as bad as starting with strangers! The key to both of these findings appeared to be that founding with people you had never done actual work with before created all sorts of problems. Instead, the most successful founders started companies with coworkers with whom they had prior experience. This allowed them a common understanding about how to work together and allowed them to experience some of the benefits of trust that come with friendship.

Surprisingly, the most successful founding team relationship was family. Though people are often advised not to start companies with family members, our data suggested that family founded companies had the highest survival rates. This might be less surprising when you think that many of the world's largest companies are still family run, from Cargill to Tata to Koch Industries, while many others, including Walmart and Ford, still have major roles for family members. This doesn't mean that founding with your loved ones is always a good idea—our research doesn't tell us what happens to families when their businesses fail—but it is at least worth considering.

Making Founding Teams Work

If you start your company with a team, as opposed to alone, you will need to put some extra effort into making the team succeed, especially at the beginning, as the members of your team will quickly become critical to the company's success.[11] There are many decisions to make among founding team members, and they need to be made as early as possible. Choices about who takes on which roles, what the goals of the team will be, how you will give each other feedback, how to handle disagreements, and many others are best sorted out before everyone has committed too much time and money.[12] The trickiest issue is likely to be dividing equity—which, if perceived as unfair by any team member, can lead to long-term resentment.[13] The process of equity division must be done thoughtfully; if you quickly divide the equity equally among a founding team, with the simple goal of avoiding any conflict, your actions may lead to worse outcomes in the future.[14] To understand why this can be a challenge, I want to give you a puzzle I commonly give to my MBA students:

> Three friends come up with an idea for a startup, and they agree they all played an equal role in coming up with the idea. They also each agree to put $10,000 in the startup. They each put the same amount of work into getting the startup off the ground, and they agree to split the work into three roles: chief executive officer (CEO), chief technology officer (CTO), and chief financial officer (CFO). These roles are equally responsible for making the company succeed, with basically the same number of hours of

responsibility and criticalness for the company's long-term success. How should these three people divide the company, in terms of the percentage of equity they should each own?

When I ask my MBAs, typically about 40% of the class wants to divide equity evenly, 33.3% for each of the three friends. This makes sense: All three people have made some important choices about what to do with their startup, they're all doing their jobs to make this happen, they're all investing equal amounts of money, and so on. A smaller group of the class divides equity equally, with some caveats, and about 20% of the class picks some rules based on assumed knowledge: This group thinks the CTO should get more equity, or the CEO should get more equity, or there should be some sort of trial by combat in which the winner decides things.

The minority of the class notices something about the case. Based on the facts that we've seen so far, it makes sense to split the equity evenly. But the problem is that the decision is based on what has happened thus far; the goal is not to motivate everyone based on what's happened in the past but to motivate everyone based on what should happen in the future. And the future holds many surprises: The company could change direction and no longer need a CFO; there may be changes in personal circumstances (someone could get sick or someone could decide to leave the job, for instance); there could be a crisis of some sort inside the organization; or, intergroup politics may lead to two of the founders turning on the third one. These are all issues that could and do happen inside organizations. You need to think not only about what *has* happened but also about your plans for the future, or what *could* happen.

How can you account for the future? For an epistemology that works for startup planning, I turn to the words of former defense secretary Donald Rumsfeld, who was himself adapting a technique called the Johari window:[15] "There are known knowns, there are things we know we know. We also know there are known unknowns . . . we know there's some things we do not know. . . . There are also unknown unknowns. The ones we don't know, we don't know." In a startup context, there are things we know that we know. We call those things facts. In the puzzle about the founding team, I only gave known knowns: The team came up with the idea together, the team decided to divide the roles evenly, and each person had put in $10,000.

But then there are also known unknowns: things that we know we don't know. What are things we know we don't know? Well, a lot of things happen in startups. We know that founders may decide to leave jobs to work full-time for the new venture. We know that founders may need to raise funds, but we don't know from whom or at what point. These are known unknowns. You know that these are uncertainties in your organization, but you also know that at some point, you will need to answer these questions. You will have to figure out how you're going to fundraise, and team members will have to decide whether to quit their jobs to join the startup. Because you know these things are going to happen, you can use contracts to address these issues. The most important type of contract is a vesting provision on the stock owned by founders. Vesting effectively means that you have to earn your equity stake over time. If you own 40% of the company, vesting over four years, you get 10% a year, but if you quit after only two years, you only walk away with 20% of the company, rather than the full amount. You can vest for reasons other than time, depending on your circumstances. For example, your vesting provision could stipulate that if somebody is working full-time at the company, they earn equity at a faster rate than someone who keeps their current job and only works for you nights and weekends. Vesting ensures that founders continue to contribute in the future, rather than being rewarded only for their initial work.

Finally, there are unknown unknowns, or things we don't know that we don't know: What if a founder has a family emergency and decides to leave your organization for six months? What if the direction of your company changes radically and a hard-working founder is no longer needed? What if a natural disaster prevents a founder from coming to work? All these things can radically change the direction of your company, but they can't be handled in contracts.

This is where building and maintaining trust among the founders is critical—only through discussion and negotiation can you handle the truly unexpected. If you are not regularly talking with the other members of your team about your underlying feelings about the company, your concerns and your worries, you are in a lot of danger. When things change, implicit agreements between people fall apart. And so you need to build trust by being open and honest and creating and maintaining an ongoing conversation about how you feel about your organization. Because smart founders who intend to work hard on their startups put considerable work into their founding agreements, those that are simply based on equal equity splits have been shown to be an indicator of a startup that is more likely to fall apart.[16]

In the next chapter, we will look at some ways to generate startup ideas.

The Founder's Checklist: Things to Remember

- There is no ideal founding personality type that works for all startups.
- Younger isn't necessarily *better* in the world of startups. The average age of a startup founder in the United States is 42.
- Having cofounders can provide some unexpected negative consequences. Going it alone (or founding with family) may be an advantage at times.
- If you have cofounders, a founders' agreement that takes into account uncertainty is a key to success.

Chapter 2

Ideas
Searching for a Light Bulb

The startup idea plays an almost mystical role in many entrepreneurial stories. Prospective founders wait anxiously for The Idea to strike. When they finally have The Idea, founders keep it secret, obsessing over it like Gollum over his ring. Eventually, they need to pitch The Idea to advisers, funders, or people like me. It is only then that they find out, almost inevitably, that their big Idea is something that has been floated many times before, or has some obvious fatal flaw. In fact, it is rare for someone to come up with a brilliant idea out of nowhere, fully formed, that is an instant winner. Most ideas are like babies, miraculous to their creators but less obviously impressive to the uninterested bystander.

As we will see in later chapters, the idea is just the start of your journey and serves as a base from which to begin the process of entrepreneurship. Over their life spans, most startups change direction, or "pivot," at least once, evolving their idea as they build out their strategy and market. But these pivots are usually variations of the initial idea, rather than an entirely new concept.

So how do you come up with a good initial idea? In this chapter, we will examine where ideas come from and how to generate good ones, separating mythical approaches from those backed by evidence.

Setting the Stage: Creativity

To come up with good ideas, you will need to be creative.

If my classes are any indication, I predict that quite a few readers responded to that sentence with either panic or annoyance, claiming that they are "not creative people." But the division between creative and noncreative people is less clear-cut than you might think. Recent research shows that among entrepreneurs, within-person differences in creativity over the course of a week are greater than across-person differences.[17] That means that maximizing your own creativity may be more important than being a "naturally creative" person. So how can you maximize your creativity?

Let's start with the basics—first, a good night's sleep is critical, as was mentioned in Chapter 1. A series of new research papers suggest that sleep is critical to successful idea generation, especially in the context of making entrepreneurs more creative.[18] The effects go beyond just creativity, however. People who are sleep-deprived not only generate lower-quality ideas but also become bad at differentiating between good ideas and bad ones. Worse still, research shows that sleep-deprived individuals become more impulsive and are more likely to act on the bad ideas they generate. That means that a chronically sleep-deprived person would be more likely to come up with bad ideas, think they are good, and suddenly quit his or her job to pursue them! So, creativity starts with a good night's sleep, and if you can't manage that, a 75-minute nap has been found to do almost as a good a job in putting people in the right frame of mind to be creative.[19]

Besides rest, what else can make you creative? Perhaps one of the most personally validating findings I have encountered suggests that coffee, or indeed any caffeine, may be helpful. Having a couple cups of coffee (or tea) significantly increases memory, creativity, and learning, with little cognitive downside.[20] Both sleep and caffeine can also help improve your mood, and it turns out that the right mood is vital to idea generation. Peppy, positive moods result in the best ideas. So staying positive and having fun in idea generation is important, though you will want to be more critical when evaluating the quality of the ideas for your startup, requiring a shift to a more serious mood.

These rules can help individuals be more creative, but many startups begin with teams of people working on an idea together, as discussed in the first chapter. Moving from creative individuals to creative teams is more complex than just scaling up the number of people. It starts with building the right group. If you are working with a number of people to generate ideas, try to assemble a group with diverse backgrounds and experiences. These types of teams are more likely to come up with new concepts than less diverse teams, who are likely to share a common point of view. Additionally, people who are good at generating ideas in one context are often good at coming up with ideas in other contexts. If you can, invite the most creative people in your network to help you generate ideas.

Additionally, how you work in your group to generate ideas matters. Rather counterintuitively, groups can actually come up with lower-quality ideas than individuals working alone. Although group brainstorming has become a cultural mainstay, the secret to starting a group idea generation session is to start it *without the group*. As soon as you start to work as a group all sorts of social processes come into play. You become self-conscious, you suppress some of your ideas to fit into the group, and you focus on what other people have to say rather than your own ideas. Groups working together generate about half the ideas of the same people working alone.[21] To obtain the greatest diversity of creative ideas, you need to start with some solo brainstorming!

Before you start talking with other members of your group, each member should take the first third of the idea sessions to write down ideas. After you have written down a list of ideas on your own you should start working with others, beginning with sharing the lists of concepts you have all generated. Alternately, everyone can pass a piece of paper with an idea or two to their right, and the next person can silently add an idea to the list, and so on. This approach, called "brainwriting," has been shown to be an effective technique for idea generation. You will then want to proceed to an open discussion of ideas with the other people in your group, giving everyone a chance to build on each other's ideas, get buy-in, and come up with new thoughts. You can do this through traditional brainstorming or using other approaches, like writing down ideas on Post-it notes, which can then be placed on the walls around the room. Combining individual and group thinking is the most powerful approach to generating ideas.

You can even generate ideas over a couple drinks. Much like caffeine, alcohol improves idea generation.[22] In studies of idea generation, intoxicated people came up with more creative ideas than their sober counterparts and were more likely to have sudden "aha" moments.[23] Furthermore, the ideas that tipsy people come up with turn out to be of higher quality, even when evaluated by (presumably sober) judges later. I wouldn't suggest making drinking a feature of your startup, however, as, outside all the obvious reasons that this might create issues, research shows that company cultures built around drinking are more likely to engage in fraud and other forms of unethical behavior.[24]

However you put yourself in a more creative space, you now need to actually come up with a good business idea, while avoiding traps and myths.

Research has shown that the way you see problems, often referred to as the *framing* of the problem, has a huge impact on the degree to which you see entrepreneurial opportunities. By changing your frame, you can come up with radical new ideas or spot problems nobody else has seen. The rest of the chapter will introduce a variety of frames—try them all! Some frames work better in some situations, but any frame might be helpful in getting you to break out of an old idea and spark a creative moment where you find a great new opportunity.

Framing Around Effectuation: Questions for You

One common mistake people make when looking for entrepreneurial ideas is starting top-down by finding a growing market and then trying to figure out how to enter it. This can work—it is how Jeff Bezos decided to launch Amazon!—but only if you are right about the potential trend, have the resources to execute the idea, and are early enough in the process that there is not too much competition. In most cases, startups that try to enter a hot market have lower performance than those that avoid chasing the latest trend.[25]

So what is the alternative to starting with this top-down approach to finding a market? Professor Saras Sarasvathy has studied dozens of successful entrepreneurs, and she realized that they had something in common. When framing their thinking around startup ideas, they started not with the goal they had in mind but rather with the means at their disposal. This approach, called "effectual reasoning," offers a powerful way for potential founders to come up with startup concepts.[26]

Effectual reasoning starts with you, as a potential founder, and requires that you ask yourself three questions:

(1) Who are you?
(2) What do you know?
(3) Who do you know?

Though these questions may seem simple, using them in practice can lead to profound results. Together, the questions ask you to consider the resources you have available to you right now and the talents and skills that can make you successful. Even more importantly, they require you to think about the markets you might know better than anyone else, as well as which markets may have needs that have been overlooked by other startups who don't have your unique combination of knowledge and abilities. Sarasvathy calls this the Bird in Hand Principle: Start with the resources you have today and leap into starting your business based on what you can do better than anyone else. Don't wait for the objectively perfect idea; embrace the idea that only you can implement right now.

This is part of why older founders are often more successful, as discussed in Chapter 1. They have more skills, resources, and knowledge about potential markets than people who have less work experience and therefore have a better chance of finding effectual startup ideas. But you don't need to be an executive with 20 years of experience to use effectuation. Approaching your skills and con- nections from an effectual perspective may let you start something that initially seems less ambitious, but which can end up launching a new industry!

Consider, for example, the story behind the rebirth of virtual reality. VR was a hot area for startups in the early 1990s, attracting investment around VR arcade machines and even primitive home VR equipment, but the market imploded by the middle of the decade. Despite the collapse of the commercial VR market, hobby- ists continued to be interested in the visual of goggles that could transport the user to computer-generated environments. One of these hobbyists was Palmer Luckey, who provides a great example of effectual entrepreneurship. To answer the three questions for Luckey:

(1) *Who are you?* A homeschooled technical genius, with curios- ity about new technologies and resources from side businesses that allowed him to access hardware with which to tinker.
(2) *What do you know?* How to build virtual reality headsets in ways nobody else can, and in ways few people are interested.
(3) *Who do you know?* Other virtual reality hobbyists on the 3-D gaming site Meant to Be Seen, plus many of the lumi- naries behind early VR efforts.

Given these resources, Luckey came up with the idea for a VR startup in an effectual way. He started by building VR devices for him- self, which he then marketed as kits to members of the hobbyist com- munities of which he was a part, attracting further attention. Based on the demand in his community, he launched a Kickstarter for $250,000 to sell his new Oculus Rift headsets. The initial buzz in his commu- nity spread, and he ultimately raised $2.4 million. Soon afterward, Facebook bought his company, Oculus VR, for about $2.3 billion, leading to a suddenly resurgent VR industry. Luckey did not start this trend by conducting a rational search for a market to enter—no one was investing in virtual reality. Instead, he started with who he was, what he knew, and the people with whom he was connected.

Framing Around Constraints: Changing the World

Another trick to generate good ideas is to change the boundaries of the problem by altering the constraints you face. This allows you to see a problem in a new way, which might lead to new solutions. The most obvious way to do this is to remove all your constraints. This has been called the "What Would Croesus Do?" approach by Professors Barry Nalebuff and Ian Ayres[27]—after the legendary ancient king who had all the money in the world. This approach asks what you would do to solve a problem if you had infinite resources, and then work backward from that special case to consider a more general solution.

For example, let's say you were rich and busy and you just dropped your new iPhone and broke it. You obviously wouldn't go to the Apple Store yourself, since malls are for "regular people." You wouldn't even want to send an assistant, as that would take valuable time during which you wouldn't have your phone. Even having a pile of new iPhones wouldn't be good enough—it still would take an hour or two to restore your backup information. Instead, you might have dedicated assistants constantly updating a new iPhone with your latest backup, just so you are ready at all times to toss aside your broken phone and start using a new one immediately. We have removed all our constraints and come up with a new approach to the problem of breaking your phone (for the very, very rich!).

Obviously, however, not everyone can afford to have assistants backing up their phones continuously, so this idea is ridiculous. Instead, we can consider how we might get the same effect without the same expense: How can we quickly give people replacement phones with their personal data after they lose theirs? We know people are already willing to pay for services like AppleCare to get their phones repaired. What if we could offer an improved service in a similar price range? We can get some of the same effects as the unconstrained example in a more reasonable way: Imagine a service that has vans with backup iPhones placed in major cities. As soon as people break their phones, they can call for a van and also securely send their account details, allowing a backup to be uploaded to a phone already waiting in the van. The van would drive to the customer, exchange the old phone for the new one, and handle the details of returning and replacing the broken phone, all for a reasonable fee. Whether this idea would be profitable is unclear, but it does illustrate how removing the constraints from a problem can lead to new ways of thinking about good ideas and spark new approaches.

Interestingly, adding constraints can have the same effects. Psychological experiments have shown that when people have limitations on the ideas they can pursue they are often, paradoxically, more creative. For example, in one study, participants were told to design a toy for children, given five weirdly shaped blocks selected from a larger set of pieces.[28] In some cases, the experimenters randomly gave people blocks, while in others they were allowed to pick their own. Additionally, in some cases, the subjects had to use all five blocks, or they were allowed to use any number of the blocks they were given. The least constrained scenario, in this case, allows for people to pick their own blocks and use whatever amount they see fit. Surprisingly, people in this group came up with the least creative answers. Instead, the most constrained group, where people were given five blocks randomly and had to use all five, was actually the most creative, both in process and outcomes. Constraints help because they force you to change your thinking and break out of old frames. You can add constraints to your ideas in various ways, often by consciously changing your perspective. For example:

- You can consider extreme users of a product or service, which can force you to think of novel angles: How would an astronaut use a common product? What about a child? Someone on the run from a secret conspiracy?

- You can place constraints on your solution to spark new approaches: What if it had to be done using an online service? How could the problem be solved by modifying an animal or plant? What if it had to be done for less than $10?
- You can consider opposites, which force you to think about the space more generally: What would you do if you were trying to make the problem worse? What is the most complex way you could solve this particular issue?

Framing by Abduction: Questions for Others

One of the most important things you can do to change your perspective is to actually observe the world and see if you can learn anything new or surprising. This involves moving past searching the internet or reading books (though please come back to this one!) and instead watching people go about an activity that you are interested in exploring for your business idea. Even better: Interview some potential customers!

Interviewing is a skill that improves with practice, but here are a few basic tips on effective approaches.

- **First, put some effort into deciding who you want to interview.** As a general rule, the best people to interview are the potential customers of your future product. For example, if you are considering a service that provides mentoring for college athletes to help them keep up their grades while playing, you would want to start by interviewing some average athletes, ideally across a few sports and schools. A second useful group to approach is extreme users, who have advanced or unusual needs. These can help you see where the market is going and look for innovations and problems you have not considered. In our example, that might include athletes who are about to go professional, athletes in unusual and time-consuming sports (like mountain climbing), or athletes at demanding schools.

- **You generally want to avoid solely talking to people with whom you have easy access unless you don't have any other choice.** And if you can't find anyone willing to talk to you, you are likely to have problems finding customers, as well, since it is often harder to locate people who want to buy your product than to have a conversation with you!

- **When you are interviewing, you should consider the questions you are asking in advance and make sure you are asking similar questions for every interview.** This allows you to make comparisons across interviews. You are trying to learn from the person you are interviewing, and the more you talk, the less you learn. You want your subjects to give you their own interpretation and thoughts, so focus on open-ended questions that solicit stories, paying attention to how people solve their own problems. You might want to ask the athletes in our example how they handle studying during tough training weeks or to tell you about a time they felt a lot of academic and athletic pressure. You can also ask your potential customers about the products they use today, discuss how they chose them, and have them walk you through how they use them. Have the athletes show you how they study, what techniques they use, and how they improvise their own solutions. Take notes! By carefully observing and listening to your potential customers, you are creating what you need in order to engage in abductive framing.

Abductive framing involves looking at the surprises you find in your observations and coming up with a common story or need that explains them. You should look for the counterintuitive: contradictions in behavior between what people say and actually do or workarounds people use to solve their problems.[29] This can lead to surprising insights.

For example, you may have observed that many athletes put substantial work into choosing courses that are both easy and that fit their schedules during the sports season and that all athletes took the same courses. They may have complained that the courses they wanted to take did not fit their needs. That might mean that your mentoring idea for students may not accommodate a real need. Instead, maybe you should create an online course that is available to travel teams by subscription, allowing them to get college credit and take required courses without needing to skip valuable lessons. Even if you do not generate a direct startup idea, the insights of this frame are often useful.

Framing for Serendipity: The Aha Moment

There is no startup angel that will descend from the heavens to give you a good idea. But that doesn't mean that ideas can't come from sudden inspiration. In fact, a study of scientists and artists found that 20% of their breakthrough ideas came while their minds were wandering, resulting in surprise "aha!" moments.[30] Good ideas may come while showering, walking a dog, or sitting under an apple tree. But to get these sorts of moments, you need to prepare by priming your brain with the right kind of knowledge to make a sudden connection. This process is called scanning, and it involves making sure you are continuously taking in new information from diverse sources. This increases the chance you will make a happy connection, take an intuitive leap, or find a question that leads you to a unique idea.

One way to scan is to use social media appropriately. An MIT study found that Twitter users who followed diverse groups of people were better at generating ideas than those with closed networks.[31] Diversity was defined as following others across different disciplines, industries, and points of view, rather than inhabiting any one particular community. You can do this by following those known as thought leaders—famous CEOs, politicians, analysts, academics, and authors in different fields. Then, look at who those thought leaders are interacting with and follow those people as well, since experts often can identify other experts. One person interviewed for the study suggested a 70/30 split: 70% of your follows should be people in your industry; 30% should be diverse or unusual viewpoints. You don't need to use Twitter to take in diverse information. You can accomplish the same thing by skimming academic journals, reading internet forums like Reddit, or even talking to people in real life. A study of startup boot camps found that potential founders who were open to new experiences generated a lot of good startup ideas when they interacted frequently with extroverted people.[32]

There are also storehouses of ideas that are available to founders, often patented ideas that may have cost millions of dollars to create. You can find these ideas in university technology transfer offices, which offer to license patented technologies created by university scientists in return for a fee or share of the profit. For example, as of early 2020, the University of Pennsylvania has 375 patents available for licensing, covering everything from gene therapy to drones to a smart yoga mat. For those with the appropriate skills, these ideas can be incredibly valuable, and universities are often eager to find qualified startups that want to commercialize their work. Even if these technologies aren't interesting to you, browsing through them can increase the chance that you find further valuable connections.

You should also make sure to take notes on what you learn. Both Gates and Virgin Group founder Richard Branson swear by note-taking as a key to startup success. Without having written notes to review regularly, you lower the chances of remembering details that are vital to sparking new ideas. Though taking handwritten notes has been proven to boost recall of the noted material, their lack of searchability can be a problem for some people, so you can simply create notes as a file on your phone. Make sure to write down facts, ideas, and fragments of concepts as they occur to you, and go back through them once a month to identify new connections. There are no guarantees in idea generation, but proper preparation increases your chance of success.

Exploring Your Idea, with Science!

This chapter is about what science can teach us about entrepreneurial ideas, but as an entrepreneur, you can also explore your own ideas scientifically. In fact, the best evidence we have about testing ideas shows that founders who use a disciplined, scientific process are more likely to succeed. Recently, a group of Italian academics conducted a randomized controlled experiment on 116 startups. Half the founders were taught how to do rigorous experiments on their startup ideas, generating hypotheses and testing them systematically. The other half was taught to do experiments but was not shown how to use the scientific method. The groups that acted like scientists did much better—pivoting more, avoiding problems, and ultimately generating higher revenues than the control group.[33] Methodical, but quick, experimentation can turn good ideas into great ones.

Although we know that a scientific approach to idea testing is important, there is no single method to applying scientific approaches to startups that has been proven to work better than others. Perhaps the most widespread of these scientific approaches is the Lean Startup Method, pioneered by Steve Blank and Eric Ries.[34] In its basic form, the Lean Startup Method proposed that the key to a successful startup involved a bias toward action. Founders start by turning the key questions they have about their business into testable hypotheses. Then they build fast and cheap Minimal Viable Products (MVPs) to test with real customers as quickly as possible. If the tests show they are correct, they proceed. If not, they pivot and change direction, modifying the product they are selling or the market they are approaching based on the feedback from their MVPs. They continue exploring combinations of product and market until they achieve a product-market fit with a demonstrated demand for their product.

The Lean Startup approach was extremely influential, changing expectations for what startups should do with their ideas by emphasizing the need to reach out to real customers as soon as possible. However, this approach also comes with potential downsides.[35] Focus on getting fast feedback from real customers to MVPs makes startups prone to aim for incremental improvements, focusing on what customers want today rather than trying to see ahead into the future. That can be hard to do if you are being innovative, as Steve Jobs noted when he said that "it isn't the customer's job to know what they want." Additionally, a lot of research shows that novelty is often initially disliked by customers. Seeking external validation from early customers can be even harder if you have a breakthrough idea than if you have an incremental, but easily explained, product.

In addition to these fundamental problems, there are some aspects of the Lean Startup approach, such as the emphasis on large numbers of customer interviews over other forms of experimentation, as well as the use of business model mapping, that resemble ritual more than science. Both are time-consuming articles of faith, rather than entirely evidence based. These concerns do not invalidate the fact that the Lean Startup Method offers significant advantages over older approaches to idea testing, especially in its emphasis on verifying ideas through action. At the same time, it's also worth looking into more recent approaches to idea testing to see if there are strategies that work better for your startup.[36]

Whether you adopt the Lean Startup or another method, the basics of the scientific approach to idea testing are similar. First, you need to figure out the sources of uncertainty in your business. This can be a challenge for founders, since they are often thinking of how their business will succeed, not obstacles in the way. But looking for unspoken assumptions is critical to startup success. In fact, that is one reason startups that engage in business planning are much more likely to survive than those that don't—the mere act of planning helps uncover potential issues with the business before you encounter them.[37] The point is to be able to understand what must be true about the world for your business idea to work, and how well you understand the factors associated with your idea's success. Business planning helps uncover what you actually know about customers' interests versus what you are assuming. There is usually a large list of these potential assumptions that you will need to narrow down to a small set of key issues.

You can use any number of tools to help you explore your idea to look for assumptions,[38] since the goal is to make sure you unearth as many hidden sources of uncertainty as possible in a methodical way. A direct way to do this is to use the list of Business Model Questions developed by Harvard Business School's Thomas Eisenmann, which covers key questions every startup must be able to answer about four core parts of their business:

(1) What value they deliver to customers;
(2) How they will manage the operations and technology of the startup;
(3) How they will market and sell the product; and
(4) How they will make money.

If you take the time to go through each question in detail with at least one other person, the resulting discussion should surface many of your key assumptions. Once you find those three to five key assumptions that are most important to your business success, you'll develop those into hypotheses.

Business Model Questions

Harvard Business School Professor Thomas R. Eisenmann's "Business Model Analysis for Entrepreneurs" lists key questions founders should be able to answer about their business, grouped in four categories.[39]

Customer Value Proposition

- What *unmet needs* will the venture serve?
- Will it emphasize *differentiation* or *low cost*?
- Which *customer segments* will it target?
- Will it serve a *new, existing,* or *resegmented* market?

- What will be the *minimum viable product* at launch? The *road map* for adding features?
- Who will provide *complements* required for a *whole-product solution*? On what terms?
- How will the product be priced? Does *skimming* or *penetration pricing* make sense?
- Can the venture leverage *price discrimination* methods? *Bundling*? *Network effects*?
- What *switching costs* will customers incur? What is the expected *life of a customer relationship*?
- Relative to rivals' products, how will customers' *willingness* to pay compare to their *total cost of ownership*?

Technology and Operations Management

- What activities are required to develop and produce the venture's product?
- Which activities will the venture perform in-house and which will it *outsource*?
- Who will perform outsourced activities, and under what terms?
- What are the *cost drivers* for key activities? Can the venture exploit *scale economies* in production by substituting fixed for variable costs?
- Will the venture create any valuable *intellectual property*? If so, how will it be kept proprietary?
- Are there other *first-mover advantages* in technology and operations (e.g., preemption of scarce inputs)? *Late-mover advantages* (e.g., reverse engineering)?
- Given capacity and hiring constraints, can the venture scale operations rapidly?

Go-to-Market Plan

- What mix of *direct* and *indirect channels* will the venture employ? What margin and/or exclusive rights will channel partners require?
- Given expected *customer lifetime value*, what *customer acquisition cost* will the venture target?

- What mix of free and paid *demand generation methods* will the venture employ? What will be the shape of its *customer conversion funnel*? The customer acquisition cost for each paid method?
- If the venture relies on free demand generation methods, what will be its *viral coefficient*?
- Will the venture confront a *chasm* between early adopter and early mainstream segments? If so, what is the plan for crossing the chasm?
- Does the venture have strong incentives to race for scale due to network effects, high switching costs, or other first-mover advantages? Do scalability constraints and late-mover advantages offset these incentives?

Profit Formula

- What *contribution margin* will the venture earn?
- What *fixed costs* will the venture incur, and what *breakeven capacity utilization and sales volume* does this imply?
- What share of the *total addressable market* does the breakeven sales volume represent?
- How much *investment* in working capital and property, plant, and equipment will be required per dollar of revenue?
- How will contribution margins, fixed costs, and investment/revenue ratios change over time?
- Given projected growth, what will be the profile of the venture's *cash flow curve*? How deep is the curve's trough, and when will it be reached?

"Summary of Business Model Questions" from "Business Model Analysis for Entrepreneurs" by Professor Thomas Eisenmann [product# 9812096]. © 2014 President and Fellows of Harvard College. Republished by permission of Harvard Business Publishing.

Hypotheses for startups, just like hypotheses in science, must do a few key things: They must test at least one of the key assumptions you surfaced, and they must be both testable and falsifiable. *Testable* means that you can build an experiment that will let you discover whether your hypothesis is right or wrong with the time and resources available to you. If your hypothesis requires you to build your full product and launch into the world, that's not testable, since you cannot run that experiment until your product is already completed. Similarly, if your hypothesis says 80% of people will love a product but you don't know how you're going to figure out whether that level of customer delight is true, that's not testable. On the other hand, a hypothesis that 5% of the potential customers emailed about a product will ask for additional information is testable. You can definitely send such an email and track the response rate.

A hypothesis also must be *falsifiable*. Entrepreneurs tend to be optimistic and see things in the best light, so you need to avoid ambiguity between good and bad results in your own hypothesis so that you don't draw the wrong conclusions. A falsifiable hypothesis avoids this problem by establishing a clear numerical threshold for what a successful test looks like. These numbers should not be arbitrary. You will need a financial model for your business that will allow you to test various scenarios to generate useful thresholds, whether those are costs (the product needs to be manufactured for less than $40) or customer acquisition rates (50% of people who come to our homepage will need to place an order for our model to work). "People will like our product," for instance, is ambiguous and not falsifiable, or even testable. "Forty percent of our customers who try the prototype will agree to preorder the product" is falsifiable and testable. If 40% of people who try the product don't agree to place an order, then your hypothesis is wrong.

Once you have your hypotheses, you can run experiments to see if they are true. The best experiments are the ones that tell you the most for the lowest cost and effort. Generally, experiments will increase in complexity and difficulty as you learn more and test deeper assumptions. Usually, founders start by interviewing potential customers and doing market research. Then they may progress to surveying, focus groups, and creating crude mockups. Next might come prototypes and working minimal viable products. Each type of experiment has its own advantages and disadvantages, and there are further resources on experimentation at *www.unicorns-shadow.com*. Simpler is usually better. If you can test key assumptions by interviewing customers versus creating an expensive prototype, then definitely interview customers first!

By systematically testing assumptions through running experiments to prove or disprove hypotheses, you can learn whether your idea will work the way you expect. If it doesn't, you can pivot—change direction for your idea based on what you learned in your experiments. Pivoting is easier early in the history of your company, so starting with cheap and fast experiments has the added advantage of helping you zero in on a winning strategy when it is still possible to alter course. Though there are many companies that have pivoted a significant amount (both Slack and Flickr, for instance, started off as video game companies), most pivots are smaller and represent more minor changes to the company's strategy.[40] In fact, being conservative can help, as recent research suggests that founders often change direction too much when pivoting.[41] Once you have begun to prove out your idea, you will need the resources to execute on it. That is where fundraising becomes critical, as we will discuss in the next chapter.

The Founder's Checklist: Things to Remember

- There is no one way to generate startup ideas, so you might want to try many approaches, but start with a good night's sleep (and maybe a cup of coffee). You can also prepare yourself for coming up with a sudden insight by monitoring the world around you.
- Use effectuation by asking, "Who am I? What do I know? Who do I know?"
- Use constraints to boost creativity.
- Find good ideas by going into the world and interviewing and observing customers, using abduction.
- The evidence strongly supports using a scientific approach to testing your ideas. Make sure to generate hypotheses from key assumptions that are testable and falsifiable, and then run experiments to improve your idea.

Chapter 3

Funding
Branching Paths

Jamie Siminoff was determined to be a successful entrepreneur, but his products were hit or miss. One of his ideas, an herbal supplement designed to improve body odor, had the unfortunate side effect of turning the user's stools green, but others made him enough money to keep inventing. He was most excited by Doorbot, a cell phone–connected doorbell, but had trouble finding investors until he had a lucky break. He was invited to appear on *Shark Tank*, the wildly popular television show that shaped how many people think of startup pitching (while making the funding process appear much more dramatic than it is).[42] Siminoff spent his last $20,000 on an elaborate set to show off Doorbot and . . . found the sharks unwilling to fund his idea.

With nothing left in his bank account, he pursued alternate approaches to funding Doorbot, including exploiting the free advertising from being on TV to sell directly to customers. Based on this early success, Siminoff raised venture capital, and the company, now renamed Ring, sold to Amazon for over a billion dollars just five years after he was rejected by the sharks.[43] The story of Ring, and the hundreds of investors who turned it down just years before it became a giant success, is a sign of how hard it is to fund winning startups, from the perspectives of both entrepreneurs and funders.

All startups want money. But not all startups need as much money as they think they do from the sources they think they need. In fact, most startups do not seek outside investors at all. An analysis of the Kauffman Firm Survey, a representative survey of US start-ups, shows that the biggest source of funds for high-growth startups, on average, are the personal savings of the founders. The second largest is debt, either personal debt or loans taken out by the new company. Friends and family come a distant third, and most companies do not have serious investors beyond that. Rather counterintuitively, research shows that startups with less money are often more successful and creative than ones that are better funded, in part because the lack of resources forces them to be more innovative.[44] But there are certain startups that need a lot of money to get off the ground, either because they require research and development before launching (like biomedical startups) or because they need to spend a large amount on marketing (like a new direct-to-consumer brand). Those startups will almost certainly need outside funds from investors.

Investors essentially fall into two categories: professional and amateur. Professional investors are primarily venture capitalists, but they may include a small subset of angel investors who put their own money into startups. Except for the rare individual who makes multiple personal investments, professionals usually manage other people's money, invest it in a wide range of startup companies, often make many investments at the same time, and can deploy large amounts of cash in making follow-on bets on successful companies. Amateur investors include everyone else, from crowdfunding partners to your aunt to less experienced angel investors. These individuals usually invest small amounts in just one company and do not follow up that initial stake with future investments. Research has shown that professional and amateur investors behave quite differently, and they need to be approached differently. What persuades a professional does not persuade an amateur, and vice versa, as we will discuss in the next chapter.

The Funding Road Map

Professional and amateur investors play different but complementary roles in the fundraising process. Amateurs tend to provide small amounts of cash during the high-risk early days of a startup, and professionals step in to deploy more money as the startup begins to prove itself. Fundraising quickly becomes a cycle: Startups raise money based on the progress they have made, they use that money to show more progress, and then they raise more capital allowing them to show further progress. The loop continues until the company is profitable or has "exited"—hopefully through an acquisition or an initial public offering, but often because it has gone out of business. A cycle in which a startup raises money is called "a round," and these rounds have informal names without fixed definitions, though they generally follow a pattern:

1. A "friends and family round" (sometimes called "pre-seed") is where founders get initial investment from people who either believe in their idea or who would feel guilty if they didn't help out. This round is usually in the $50,000–$500,000 range, depending on the business (and the net worth of your friends and family). The money is enough to build early mockups and start to work on your idea, with the goal of raising further seed funding. As we will see shortly, crowdfunding can also play a role as an alternative to the friends and family round, as can accelerators.

2. The "seed round" is when serious investors start to put money into your company, and this usually involves angel investors, whether professional or amateur. However, other approaches, like crowdfunding or seeking government grants, can be helpful at this stage as well, especially for smaller seed rounds. The seed round is usually under $1.5 million, and the goal with seed money is to show that you can get real customers interested in your product and that they are willing to pay for it. With that proof in hand, you can raise an A round.

3. The "A round" (or "series A") is the first round of investment for venture capital and usually provides under $5 million in funding, which is too much for most angels to afford. Typically,

the goal is to start scaling the business, or to build a final product so that you can then raise a B round.

4. "B rounds," "C rounds," and so on are the follow-on investments, each for an escalating amount (Uber raised a series G round!). This often involves the same venture capitalists as your A round, plus new investors. On average, at this stage, companies raise capital every year and a half to two years to sustain their growth in a quest to go public.

The sequencing of rounds seems like a road map, with one leading to the next. But that feeds into a particularly dangerous fundraising myth that suggests raising as much capital as possible is a good thing. This is far from the truth. Every time you raise capital, with a few exceptions, you will give away part of your company (your equity) and you will likely also give away some decision-making power, including seats on your board of directors. This transfer of power can be a small price to pay if you need money, but eventually this process of "dilution" can leave founders with very little stake in their own company, and even get them fired (over half of founders are replaced as CEOs by the C round of funding!).[45]

There are also other potential downsides to fundraising. Seeking funds is a time-consuming affair, one that takes months of intense work from founders. Even after a funder is interested, it takes an average of 83 days to close a venture capital deal. During this time, a founder's attention is often focused on fundraising rather than other critical aspects of the venture. With that warning out of the way, we can turn to the specifics of fundraising and the myths and evidence around different approaches to fundraising.

Initial Investments: Crowds, Friends, and Family

The first source of outside money for most founders is friends and family. Approaching your network first makes sense because the risk of rejection is lower and their willingness to trust you is higher. But raising friends and family money does come at a psychological cost.

Many founders are reluctant to let down people to whom they are close, while they may not feel the same way about investors who are only interested in financial returns. This can lead to considerable stress, which plays out in early decisions startups make. Research has shown, for example, that founders who take money from family members are much less likely to take risks than those who get investment from strangers.[46]

There are alternatives to friends and family money in the early stages of a startup, including seeking loans or government grants. For many startups, however, the most accessible and useful form of early cash comes from crowdfunding. Crowdfunding refers to a variety of ways to pool relatively small contributions from large numbers of people on the internet. The most popular format, reward crowdfunding, is commonly done on sites like Kickstarter and Indiegogo. It involves offering a reward in the future in return for a contribution today. This can range from a product (as we saw earlier, Oculus Rift was crowdfunded), to a new album, to a walk-on part in a movie. Reward crowdfunding works best for physical goods (technological gadgets, clothes, unique products, artwork, and board games are all popular with crowdfunders, for instance) and for creative work with a tangible output (like movies, albums, and books). Sites like Patreon have extended the reward crowdfunding model to supporting artists and creators, by allowing fans to become "patrons" of creators they like and pay a monthly fee for access to exclusive content. There are other ways of crowdfunding, including offering equity, but those tend to be less common for entrepreneurs and usually work in more specialized cases. For most people seeking crowdfunding to launch a business, reward crowdfunding is the right approach.

One of the first challenges facing anyone launching a crowdfunding campaign is deciding on a dollar goal. On many sites, like Kickstarter, the project must achieve the goal to receive any money. Founders often think they should set the crowdfunding goal as low as possible and then hope to achieve a large multiple (as Oculus Rift did when it raised over $2 million, even though its goal was only $250,000). Founders believe a low goal and a large multiple will impress funders, but my research shows otherwise. In my surveys of tens of thousands of crowdfunding creators, I found that the amount of money raised in crowdfunding did predict which companies would later attract venture capital, but the multiple over the goal didn't matter at all. Plus, there is an additional downside to setting too low a goal. Most crowdfunding projects either fail by a lot or succeed by a little. Only 1% of all crowdfunding projects get 10 times their initial goal, and entrepreneurs who try to game the system by setting a low goal may find themselves stuck with a small amount of money and an obligation to the people who backed them. When setting your goal, it's best to estimate the realistic amount you think you will need to produce your product.

Beyond goal setting is a plethora of additional work. Successful crowdfunders lay the groundwork for success long before they launch their project. I found that most successful founders spend between 10 and 25 hours a week preparing the campaign for weeks in advance of the launch of their crowdfunding projects. They start by examining other successful campaigns, using those to create well-written descriptions of their product, and producing high-quality videos central to any pitch. My research showed this work made a difference. Not only did preparation lead to success but the crowd can be picky—a single spelling error in the campaign's text is linked to a 13% lower chance of success for the project!—so developing and testing a pitch, which we will describe in more detail in the next chapter, is particularly vital.

Successful crowdfunding creators also reach out to potential customers to preview their campaigns. My research has shown that crowdfunding does start with family and friends—most of the initial investment comes from people you know—but it also allows others to get involved. Rather than relying on venture capitalists and marketers to get your product, creators can directly reach out to customers and communities to refine ideas and gauge interest. Establishing these connections is vital because crowdfunding transforms the normally limited market for early stage fundraising, making it a more open process by connecting creators and entrepreneurs directly with customers and funders. Crowdfunding acts as a platform, matching innovators with those who need innovation, and thus is reshaping which ideas come to market.

Connections also matter because money is just part of what a platform like crowdfunding provides. My surveys of successful crowdfunders show that raising money is not the most important goal of many crowdfunding efforts. Instead, crowdfunding serves to validate demand and build communities of support. In the case of Oculus, crowdfunding acted as a platform that allowed Palmer Luckey's enthusiastic community of VR hobbyists to directly support one of their own, making Oculus a reality without needing to go through traditional gatekeepers. This establishes a direct connection between the project creator and the funder. The community backing the project often comes to feel a sense of ownership for the projects it supports. This ownership is typically quite positive, as it can lead to communities creating complementary products (such as apps that use a new crowdfunded technology) and promotional support. The pressure of community support also instills a sense of obligation in project creators. As a result, despite the limited ramifications of failure for project creators, the vast majority of projects make good on their promises; only about 9% of projects fail to deliver, and creators can go through extraordinary efforts, such as spending their own money, to fulfill promises to backers. The relatively low failure rate highlights the personal connections provided by platforms, but that connection can be problematic: If money is given as an impersonal investment (such as from an angel investor), a founder whose first startup fails due to factors outside his or her control may still receive VC funding in the future. But project creators who do not deliver to their backers are likely to find a less forgiving audience.

Crowdfunders, despite not being handpicked experts, have the ability to identify talented projects. Research I have conducted with Professor Ramana Nanda of Harvard Business School shows they are often at least as good at making decisions as experts. Crowdfunding has eclipsed the National Endowment of the Arts as a source of funding for the arts, a subject of considerable concern to critics who worried that crowds would favor low-culture crowd-pleasers over serious theater (more musicals about dancing cats, less experimental work). Together, Professor Nanda and I examined whether the crowd and experts agreed or disagreed on what to fund by asking professional critics to evaluate projects on Kickstarter. We found that the crowd and experts largely agreed, and, when they did not, the crowd was more likely to take a chance on projects than experts. Further, the projects the crowd (but not the experts) supported ultimately produced a higher number of critical and commercial hits than the projects that the experts approved.

The ability of crowdfunding to direct money to founders who are likely to be successful is one of the reasons crowdfunding really can help launch companies. My research has found that every dollar given to projects via Kickstarter resulted in a mean of $2.46 in additional revenue outside Kickstarter, suggesting that crowdfunding is a useful way to potentially avoid future fundraising. But if you do want to raise future funds, crowdfunding success validates that there is demand for your product. I found that 11% of all projects on Kickstarter raised outside funds, with 6% or so receiving venture capital—the vast majority of which are not in industries generally funded by VCs. It is therefore worth at least considering crowdfunding as an early source of money, and one that can lead into more standard forms of fundraising, like angels and accelerators.

Getting Serious: Angels and Accelerators

In most cases, the first outside nonfamily investment in startups comes from angels: amateur, wealthy investors who are interested in putting money into startups. Angels are not a formal group but rather a wide range of people. Many of them are former entrepreneurs who find startup investment to be interesting or exciting.[47] Most also aren't very good at it, as the vast majority of angels lose money on their investments, and, unlike venture capitalists, they cannot spread their money around across as many startups. AngelList, a leading platform that matches investors with startups, studied thousands of startups raising money from angel investors. It found that less than 10% of angels picking companies to invest in outperformed a fund that invested in every possible angel investment.[48]

What do angels look for in companies in which they invest? Interestingly, the most important characteristic is trustworthiness. Angels invest money into a company very early in the process, when there is often little evidence about whether the startup is even real. Angels will therefore often seek assurances that they can trust the founder to be a good steward of their money, and use it in ways that will lead to success. They also rely on "gut feel," or intuition, as their guide, rather than emphasizing formal analysis.[49] This changes somewhat when angels become part of angel groups that invest together and collectively make decisions that look more like venture capital investments.[50] Considering how angels make decisions can help you make a more persuasive case to early investors, as we will see in the next chapter.

There are two other major funding and support mechanisms you can use in the early stages of your startup: incubators and accelerators. Incubators have been around since at least the 1950s. They are a way of trying to get early stage startups the support they need to succeed. Usually, incubators are open to some subset of individuals. For instance, universities or regions might have an incubator, a space that provides individuals with support and (often) real estate, resources, lectures, and mentoring help. Incubators will help startups get through the early stages of their growth.

Accelerators, who also focus on early stage startups, have a different goal. They are money-making ventures and they grew out of the need to make money in an environment where the costs of starting a company has been dropping, making it harder for large investors to deploy money into a startup and get the kind of returns they want. Graham, for instance, had the idea to invest in companies before they have achieved success, even before they have a fully fleshed-out idea. The result was Y Combinator, the first accelerator, and the concept soon spread. In return for joining the accelerator, founders give up a small stake of their company in return for a mix of money and resources. These are usually intense, three- or four-month programs, with a group of other startups going through the accelerator at the same time, at the end of which founders present a public pitch to investors. With their mix of educational programs and resources, good accelerators have been shown to help founders get an edge over the competition.[51]

There are now hundreds of accelerators, but they are not all the same—there is pronounced status hierarchy.[52] The best accelerators, like AngelPad and Y Combinator, have their pick of which startups they want to have join them, with a low percentage of acceptance rates. Other accelerators take those that may not have made it into these programs. This turns out to be the key to whether you should join an accelerator. Though some lower-status accelerators can be useful if they match your strategy, high-status accelerators are usually worth joining, especially if you do not have a lot of founding experience.[53] These sorts of accelerators can give you access to high-end entrepreneurial networks and the venture capitalists that operate within them. In fact, 28% of all VC investment now comes through accelerators.[54]

The Final Form: Apex Predators and the Myth of the All-Knowing Venture Capitalist

As you can see from the progression of funding rounds, venture capitalists play a special role in the startup ecosystem. They are the only funders to provide large amounts of money to ambitious startups. This is often referred to as "rocket fuel," since it is only useful to rockets—fast-growing startups with big ambitions to take over the world. Venture capital represents a relatively small amount of global investment—the total amount of all venture capital money under management in the United States is less than the amount of money managed by the 50th largest mutual fund—but VC investment plays an important role in the overall economy. Without VCs fueling startups, US economic growth would be 28% lower![55] And for startups that need millions of dollars to launch their businesses, VCs can be indispensable. Research looking at pairs of similar companies, in which one receives venture capital and the other does not, finds that raising venture capital increases the chance of a successful exit by between two and six times.[56]

As the apex predator in the funding food chain, venture capitalists are also mythologized and admired. The most prominent venture capitalists headline conferences, write books, and offer sometimes incorrect, often inscrutable, Twitter advice. Journalist Casey Newton aptly parodied the discrepancy: "VCs in real life: *hello.* VCs on Twitter: *Success is a raft made out of tears. Obstacles are lovers in disguise. A startup is a wish your heart makes.*"[57] This benign wisdom hides a secret: Experts like venture capitalists are not really any better at predicting which early stage companies will succeed than any other reasonably informed individual.

A few years ago, a group of researchers conducted an interesting experiment at a startup pitch competition in Nigeria.[58] Each startup was rated by three different groups: startup experts like VCs and entrepreneurship professionals, panels of economists, and a machine learning system. Assuming the startup was good enough to make it to the initial pitch competition—a sign of basic quality—none of three groups did much better than random chance at predicting which startups would eventually be successful. This study, among others, strongly suggests that it is extremely hard to pick winners in startups' early days.

So how do venture capitalists earn their reputation, and, perhaps more importantly, why do some VCs seem to make so much money? Part of the answer is due to a neat social trick, and the rest is due to the ways VCs make money. The social trick was described by Professors Ramana Nanda, Sampsa Samila, and Olav Sorenson.[59] They found that venture capitalists who found an unexpected hit, like identifying Facebook or Uber as great investments before anyone else did, usually never got lucky again. This is because predicting winners among early stage startups is difficult. However, because they found a lucky investment opportunity, the rest of the startup world *believed* that the investor had special insight. Going forward, founders sought out this "insightful" investor, because an investment from this investor is not just an investment—it is a sign of success. Founders are willing to take up to 14% lower valuations to get high-prestige investors to put money into their companies.[60] This means that the lucky venture capitalist not only has the best companies lining up to receive investment from him or her but also does so at a discount. It's a virtuous cycle (for the VCs at least!): VCs who have been lucky in the past continue to make money in the future, reinforcing their status as winners.

But social status is only one way VCs can turn a profit. The other approach has been nicknamed "spray and pray" and involves making lots of small risky bets on many startups as early as possible.[61] VCs can't really make money on these tiny investments, since they run funds with hundreds of millions of dollars. Instead, in these initial investments, VCs establish what are known as *pro rata rights*. Pro rata rights allow venture capitalists to continue to invest in your company in the future if they have made an initial investment. By making many small investments, VCs are essentially taking options on the future success of a startup. They can pump more money into the successful ones and drop the underperforming ones. This is another reason why venture capital can be dangerous to startups. Once you have investment from a venture capitalist, you better hope they invest in future rounds, since everyone knows that VCs make money by doubling down on successful companies. Otherwise, it's a bad signal to other investors about the viability of your future venture.

Big Game Hunter: How to Get Venture Capital

Many startups believe hustle alone can get you meetings with VCs, but the truth is quite different. Venture capitalists are (for most intents and purposes!) people, and getting their attention and interest is inherently a social process. In fact, one reason investors put their money into VC funds is because their networks of startups are not as good as those that the VCs generate. These investors expect the venture capitalist to do the hard work of going out and sourcing founders that are good financial bets. As a result, over half of a typical VC workweek is spent networking to find investment opportunities.[62]

Founders can't simply email venture capitalists to get a meeting—a response is unlikely. VCs generally only respond to "warm" introductions, or those that come through trusted connections. Cold pitches are 16 times less likely to get funding than warm ones.[63] Getting a warm introduction makes sense for VCs, since it ensures someone else has already vetted your company and can act as a test to see whether a startup can make the right connections. If you don't have warm introductions, you will need to get them, and, unfortunately, there is no magic way to do so. Using LinkedIn contacts, friends, customers, school connections, and networking events can all help. This is also where accelerators can be useful, as evidence shows that being part of accelerators helps you meet VCs.[64] You need someone willing to email a venture capitalist and say they vouch for you, or you are unlikely to make much progress.

Assuming you can generate warm introductions, how do you get a VC deal? VCs are picky. For each single investment, they consider 101 possible companies, meet with the management of 28, go through serious reviews with the partners of 10, and do due diligence on five.[65] How do you become the chosen one? The easiest way is to have already raised venture capital. If you aren't lucky enough to have done that, there is another method that is just as effective, but it takes more work.

Professors Ben Hallen and Kathy Eisenhardt studied a variety of startups and developed a multistep process that led to VC investment.[66] The initial goal is generate as many potential contacts as possible, a step they call "casual dating." During the casual dating phase, you take advantage of your warm introductions to make connections to as many venture capitalists as possible in brief coffee-like meetings. The goal is not to have a purely social conversation, nor is it to ask for funding; instead, it is to establish relationships that you can draw on further in the process. A good way to do this is to ask potential funders for advice about strategy. And, ideally, such inquiries should make you look good. ("Which of these two exciting customers should I prioritize?" not "Which of these two bad employees should I fire?"). Once you have these contacts, you can keep them informed of your successes in the future, building up a reputation for when you actually need funding.

As that time approaches, you want to engage in what Hallen and Eisenhardt call "proof point timing," sharing a steady stream of good news with VCs right before you ask them for money. This can be sales, news articles, awards, new products, and more. Getting this all to hit at once can be challenging and may involve speeding up some initiatives and slowing down others, but it increases funder interest. You also need to understand the funders themselves. Using contacts from your casual dates, research, and connections to other entrepreneurs, you should be able to develop an idea of which funds are interested in what kinds of startups and why. You use that information in your final stage, where you set up structured competition among funders. You do this by lining up alternative ways of funding, so you don't necessarily need venture capital. Then you start by approaching less desirable investors first to generate interest you can use to get higher-status VCs onboard, ideally creating competition that will increase the value of your offer. All this culminates in a convincing pitch to your investors, which we will discuss in detail in the next chapter.

How Bias Affects Fundraising

We'd all like to believe the best ideas get funded. But fundraising is a social process, and like any social process, it is subject to all kinds of bias and other barriers that affect some people more than others. For example, since VCs must be able to meet founders and monitor their portfolio companies, most of their investments are extremely local, within just 80 miles of their headquarters.[67] And because most venture capital is concentrated in a few places in the world (with

Silicon Valley being far and away the leading location), many start-ups have to physically move to hope to get funding.[68]

But other biases are based less on practical concerns and more on the people making decisions. This is especially true in entrepreneurship, because it's difficult to know in advance which startups are going to win and which ones aren't. So, decision makers looking at which startups to support use a hard-to-quantify mix of real data, intuition, and pattern recognition.[69] As a result, lots of potential biases creep into this decision-making process. Many of those biases are unconscious, and that makes them even harder to detect.

One of the largest sources of bias is gender. Women make up 38% of business owners in the United States, but only 5–8% of venture capital money goes to companies with female cofounders.[70] This is despite the fact that female entrepreneurs perform at least as well as men once funded.[71] There are many causes for this. Women may be discouraged from attempting entrepreneurship, either because of subtle cultural expectations or because of family obligations.[72] Women also start more retail- and food-related companies, industries where venture capital has historically invested less. But even when women start companies, they have trouble getting funding relative to men.

Some of this reality is due to a combination of history and sociology. The majority of VCs have been white males. A basic principle of sociology is homophily: People like people who are like themselves, so men tend to associate with other men. As a network starts to form, it consists mostly of people who look like each other, not out of conscious discrimination but due to unconscious bias. That makes it harder for a woman to enter a network that evidence shows is largely about informal connections and warm introductions—even if entrepreneurs are looking to get access to such a network, and even if venture capitalists are looking to fund more female entrepreneurs. They look around and say, "I don't know any female entrepreneurs." Well, that's because their network is formed by this homophily principle. They tend to know other people who are like themselves, and they never get to meet the female entrepreneurs who are being successful because they're not part of their network. In research I conducted with NYU professor Greenberg, we found that this situation can reverse when even a small percentage of women begin to actively help other women get funding.[73] Recent efforts to create more women-led venture capital firms might help expand access.

The bias against female founders goes beyond just network access. Even in meetings with VCs, women are treated differently: They are asked different questions than men, with the inquiries of female founders focusing on how they will prevent loss rather than achieve gains.[74] Additionally, a research paper that I wrote with my Wharton colleague Valentina Assenova shows that at least some of the cause of the funding gap is due to men being less willing to fund female startups. We examined 27,082 people playing the Startup Game, a simulation I developed that puts university students in the roles of founders and funders of new startups and lets them make deals with each other.[75] We found that the women received 11% lower valuations (they give up more shares and get less money) for their fictional startups than men in the same class. Women and men were randomly assigned roles as funders or founders of premade companies, so the degree to which they want to start companies or what kinds of companies they start can't explain this. We can also rule out other causes for bias, as we found that men and women are equally likely to make deals with each other, and they don't differ in negotiating ability. The simple answer seems to be that male investors value female-run companies less than those run by men. (There was no bias from women!) We then looked at games that had more or fewer women playing. For every 1% more female VCs in the game, female founders raised 272% more. The percentage of female VCs was the key to closing the gap in the game, suggesting again that getting more women as VCs is a potential solution.

Though there is less research on the causes, there are also funding gaps associated with African American and Hispanic entrepreneurs as well, so biases extend across multiple disadvantaged groups.[76] The good news is that there's recognition in the entrepreneurship community that entrepreneurship must be more accessible to women and minority group members, and initiatives and groups are appearing with increasing speed. Golden Seeds, for example, is a female-run angel network focused entirely on female-led startups seeking seed money. It has invested over $120 million so far. It can be useful for founders in underrepresented groups to find like-minded individuals to help with networking and funding access. And if you're a funder looking to fund entrepreneurs, there's a real opportunity there to fund more female and minority entrepreneurs—not just because it is the right thing to do but also because investing in underrepresented groups can provide an innovative edge that allows you to reach new audiences and opportunities other founders can't locate.[77]

In the next chapter, we will discuss the pitch, which is the way you ultimately convince funders to back you.

The Founder's Checklist: Things to Remember

- The funding process proceeds in distinct stages, but you should only raise funding if it fits your strategy.
- Consider using alternative financing techniques, like crowdfunding, to avoid giving up equity in your company.
- Accelerators can be a good choice, especially if they are of high status.
- Venture capital is rocket fuel for fast-growing companies, but it comes at a cost. If you want VC, you will need to execute on a careful strategy to increase your chance of success.
- There are potential biases against female and minority founders, but those founders can also find insights and opportunities that others cannot.

Chapter 4

Pitching
Talking Your Startup into Existence

In the beginning, a startup is just words. As the influential orga-nizational theorist Karl Weick and colleagues put it, a business is "talked into existence."[78] You need to tell investors what your company does before it does anything. You need to tell potential custom-ers about the benefits of your product before anyone is actually getting those benefits. You need to convince employees to join you on your journey when that journey has barely begun.

This is the art of pitching, and a substantial amount of recent research has studied how startups can "pitch" their ideas to differ-ent groups to achieve their goals.

Successful pitching literally changes minds. A recent study put investors into MRI machines and examined their brains as they heard startup pitches. When the investors' brains lit up at a pitch, indicating neurological engagement, they were much more likely to invest.[79] Similarly, researchers have found that pitches that take advantage of the way the human brain works, including its cogni-tive shortcuts and biases, are more likely to succeed.

If you want to found a company but are not that comfortable speaking in front of people, there's a hard truth: There's no way around founder pitching. But there are a couple ways to get more comfort-able with the process:

(1) You can get better with practice and training! Controlled studies show that learning how to pitch (as we will discuss

in this chapter) actually improves how much investors are willing to back you.[80]

(2) The things you think are bad about your speech may actually make them more persuasive. Style does not always win over substance in the world of startups.

The Myths of Style

The perfect pitch is a myth. There is no one pitch for all audiences, and what you likely think of as the perfect pitch is actually not very persuasive. The passionate entrepreneur delivering a brilliant and visionary pitch to an audience of professional investors is likely to lose to a more boring, more organized speech.

The most influential technology pitch of all time started with the following stirring words: "The research program that I'm going to describe to you is quickly characterizable by saying, if in your office, you as an intellectual worker were supplied with a computer display, backed up by a computer that was alive for you all day and was instantly responsible . . . responsive . . . instantly responsive to every action you had, how much value could you derive from that?"[81]

It makes your heart race, I am sure! But this pitch actually became known as the "Mother of All Demos" and ended with a standing ovation. In the talk, Douglas Engelbart, the early computer pioneer, introduced the first use of the computer mouse, windows, word processing, video conferencing, file editing, and much more, all in 1968! Today we would say that this pitch was low on passion but high on preparedness. Preparedness is about pitches that have substance, thought and flow, are logical and laid out clearly. A passionate pitch is energetic, exciting, and highly interactive. Audiences that value preparedness may not appreciate passion, and vice versa.

According to studies, professional investors don't seem to care at all about passion—it has no impact on their willingness to invest.[82] The conventional wisdom is that founders should give peppy, positive pitches, but recent research suggests this may be a mistake—overly peppy and positive pitches can actually backfire. Pitches for innovative startup ideas that were more negative in tone were more likely to raise money—they were viewed as more realistic and analytical.[83] Professionals can see past the surface of a pitch and compare it to thousands of other startups they have seen. Flashy aspects are much less important; instead, investors are looking for signs the startup will be able to accomplish its goals. So it's not surprising that preparedness is the key to getting investment.[84] On the other hand, amateur investors and angel investors seem to care a lot more about passionate pitches because they're making less professional judgments. They want to see signs that the founder is excited about his or her company and are more likely to be swayed by charisma and passion.[85]

Surface style only goes so far, and experts at pitching consider deeper goals for their pitches—namely, how they want to change the minds of the people listening. Researchers have found that entrepreneurial pitching is a high-wire act between two chasms.[86]

On one side, founders need to appear rational and reasonable—what sociologists call "legitimate," a taken-for-granted part of the market.[87] For example, taxis have long been a legitimate way to get around, while Uber has recently become legitimized, but a service that would offer riders piggyback rides to their destinations would not be seen as legitimate. Legitimacy also comes from having well-prepared pitches.[88] It is important to be seen as legitimate, because that implies that your startup is pragmatic—likely to succeed, find customers, and avoid regulation. But it also means your product is boring, can be easily copied, and is unlikely to be, well, the next Uber.

That introduces the second chasm: distinctiveness. Startups are distinct when they are different from anything else on the market. Investors love people they see as visionaries, as it implies that their startups will have less competition and will be better positioned to take a large portion of the market in a short time, thus opening up the possibility of offering giant returns. But distinct startups may not be legitimate. That's the trap: Startups need to appear both visionary and legitimate to succeed.

Startups can use a variety of cognitive tricks to manage this problem, by emphasizing legitimacy some of the time and vision for other aspects of their businesses.[89] For example, consider cricket flour, a flour substitute made entirely from ground-up crickets. Cricket cookies sound pretty radical, so a good pitch would make it seem more legitimate. But there are also aspects of the business that are boring—making money by selling products at a low margin in the grocery store. And so, when focusing on that narrow part of the business, it would be worthwhile to emphasize a more visionary strategy. By thinking about how to balance passion and prepared-ness, and legitimacy and vision, founders can make more persuasive pitches.

Elevator Pitches

The elevator pitch is the first pitch to master. Elevator pitches are short descriptions of your business that you can give if you don't have a lot of time to go into a full business plan description—say, if you're in an elevator. To really think about an elevator pitch, you must think about why you're bothering to do one. You might have a 100-page business plan in your mind or written down. There's no way that a 20- or 30-second description of your business will be enough to convince people to give you money, or immediately, have another meeting. But you can hope to start a conversation that continues after you leave that elevator.

How do you know when someone asks you the right question? Well, questions like, "Oh, you have time to do that?" or "Where did you come up with that idea?" are not questions that get to the heart of your business. What you want is a question that shows someone understands your pitch and can follow up. Founders can use various rhetorical tricks to help make these pitches more persuasive.

The first tool you have to persuade people about your business is the analogy. The shortest possible elevator pitch for your startup is known as a high-concept pitch, and it draws less from Silicon Valley and more from Hollywood. The high-concept pitch is a way of sum-marizing a complex script for a movie in three words, using the power of analogy. This is best illustrated with an apocryphal tale told of filmmaker Ridley Scott.[90] He was proposing a daring thriller in which an extraterrestrial beast hunted humans. He managed to convince studios to invest in his movie by referencing the prior year's blockbuster. *Alien* was simply *"Jaws* in space." In three words, he managed to evoke what the movie would be about: a hunter with sharp teeth, picking off disbelieving humans one at a time until only the protagonist was left for the daring final showdown. The analogy does a lot of work.

In the same way, startups use analogies to launch their own businesses. One way to do this is by using your own high-concept pitch. LinkedIn's high-concept pitch (a "Facebook for professionals") works because it instantly communicates the complexities of a social network and the reasons it addresses a different market than Facebook. The original Tesla Roadster is an "Electric Ferrari," an analogy so potent that you know the cost of the car (expensive), the target demographic (middle-aged men), its speed (fast), and even the colors in which it will be available (definitely red). This is so common that there was a whole category of startups that defined themselves as "Uber for X": Uber for dog walkers (Wag), Uber for doctors (Zocdoc), Uber for helicopters (which is now just a branch of Uber), and even Uber for ice cream (Mix 'N' Match). Where powerful analogies work, they can make instant connections that are extremely valuable.

Another important rhetorical tool is to take advantage of categories. Humans think in categories, and research shows placing your startup within the right one can have huge advantages.[91] Consider Kodak, the photography company that saw its fortunes fade with the advent of digital cameras (which it invented first, but did not commercialize). In 2018, Kodak's stock price went up 70% in a single day, because it unexpectedly announced that it was now a blockchain company that would sell KodakCoin cryptocurrency and KashMiner computer mining tools.[92] This sudden recategorization changed the way people viewed Kodak, and, for a brief time, completely changed how it was valued.

Sudden pivots to cryptocurrency aside (though there are plenty of startups doing that!), founders can carefully choose what other products they are compared to, with large implications for their long-term success. For example, one study tested the idea of an imaginary food scanner app that would use an attached spectrometer to give the exact nutritional content of any food at which it pointed.[93] Scientists developed two different ads, one that called this device a "calorie counter" and the other a "smart food analyzer." By categorizing it as something new, customers' willingness to pay was much higher.

However, categories can also introduce negatives. Startups that categorized themselves as "disruptive" create a trade-off. Disruptive companies appear more visionary, which increases the likelihood they will secure funding. But disruption also seems less pragmatic, which discourages people from investing a lot of money into a high-risk venture. Indeed, a study of Israeli startups found that companies that called themselves disruptive were more likely to get funded, but they also received less funding than startups in other categories.[94]

The most powerful rhetorical strategy in an elevator pitch is to show proof that a startup is actually achieving its goals, because, more than anything else, it can provide much-needed legitimacy. Ideally, this is done by showing "traction"—that the startup has customers and that it is growing exponentially. In an ideal world, all startups can demonstrate this using the scientific approach to idea testing discussed in Chapter 2, but that is not always the case. Instead, startups can give a demonstration of a product as a form of proof. A good demo, like the Mother of All Demos, shows your product is real and legitimate.

Failing all that, there is always social proof—the words of others demonstrating that a product is real and powerful. Ideally, these are early customers singing your praises, but prominent figures can help as well. Would you invest in a company that legendary VC John Doerr said would be "bigger than the Internet," Ethernet inventor Bob Metcalfe called "almost as big as cold fusion," and Jeff Bezos said "was so revolutionary, you would have no problem selling it"?[95] Congratulations. You just invested in Segway, the electric scooter company. Social proof can be powerful, but it has limits!

Pitch Decks

Pitching is a remarkably formalized affair. This is not because of any immutable law but rather because of social conventions, many of which change over time. In the late 1990s, common practice was to send venture capitalists a business plan, a document that could run hundreds of pages. To be clear, nobody really read the material, and, according to research from 2009, a business plan's content seemed to have no impact on funding choices of VCs.[96] Instead, presenting a business plan was a necessary formality that would lead to more informative meetings with investors. Today, business plans have long been out of style: The current funding environment calls for Power-Point presentations known as pitch decks, which can either be presented or emailed. By 2030, the style might be for singing telegrams or virtual reality experiences—it's impossible to know. The substance and goal of the pitch is the same, but the format matters: It acts as a signal to investors that you have done the work to pass the initial screening.

For now, however, you should plan on sending or presenting slides in 10 categories for an early stage company. The average seed-stage company sends a 19-page deck via email and uses slightly fewer slides in presentations.[97] And, of course, depending on the context, the nature of the pitch will change as well. But the rough content of the slides, and the 10 topics they cover, are likely to be in any pitch.

A presentation's beginning must be engaging so audience members pay attention, and it should provide a signpost, a signal that tells them what the rest of the presentation is going to be about. You can do this by explaining the **company's purpose** in a compelling way. How you do that depends a lot on what your startup does and where you are in the process, but a good choice is to lead with a story.

Stories are a powerful way to start a presentation and they can help show the need for what you're doing. Research has shown that storytelling can play a critical role in startup success.[98] One paper identified four main types of stories founders tell.[99] Founders can tell autobiographical tales of how they came up with the idea or the need, which help establish an emotional connection with the audience. This is particularly compelling if the story can help introduce the problem and explain why the founding team is the right one to solve the problem. (For a hypothetical example: "As a doctor, I nearly lost a patient because of a bad drug interaction, something that happens thousands of times a day, and, as one of the top researchers in the field, I vowed to fix the problem.") Founders also tell visionary stories about how they will transform the future. A visionary story can highlight both expertise and need. ("Today, most restaurateurs don't understand the margins around their own dishes, but our product will ensure that in three years, 90% of them will, cutting down food waste and increasing profitability.") Market stories highlight the reception that a product is getting from customers, showing traction. ("One of our first customers took me aside to tell me that the product has increased performance by 20% and that she can't stop talking about it.") Finally, strategy stories show how a company has the resources it needs to execute. ("We learned a lot from working with our two famous investors, including how we can outsell our biggest competitor if we focus on our better user interface.")

Now that you've hooked your audience, the next step is to introduce the **problem** you'll be solving. This is the customer need you're going to address. Cleverly setting up the problem establishes your competition and story in critical ways. Let's imagine Tesla pitching its first electric car. It could set up the problem to focus more on people having an unfilled need for high-end zero emission vehicles— or on people needing sports cars with faster acceleration. The first suggests a story built around environmental friendliness, with competitors like the Toyota Prius; the second is a story about raw power, with competitors like Ferrari and Porsche. Of course, you can tell a story of environmental friendliness and of power, but for early stage startups, it is hard to have too many messages at once. Instead, it is easier to emphasize a single key problem. In any case, you want to provide data on how you know the problem exists, ideally from research you have conducted to show that you understand your market.

You then move on to the **solution**, or how you solve the problem. As a side benefit, it also shows you've created something real and tested it (which you hopefully have done by the time you're pitching potential investors). The nature of the solution will depend on how you set up the problem, but it should be a direct response to the issues you raise in the problem slide. Interestingly, the solution slide is the one investors spend the *least* time looking at, since the best solutions should feel like sudden revelations, which you will address with more complexity later in the pitch.[100] You also might want to consider a demonstration here.

The fourth key slide is your **magic** (sometimes called the **why now** slide). What you do in your magic slide depends a lot on your startup, but the goal is to show you have some sort of unfair competitive advantage over other people. The ideal form of magic is that your product is already working in the market, showing that you have traction. And the best form of traction is to show exponential growth in your sales or use, though this is often a challenge. Other forms of magic can include proprietary technology, indications that you are entering at an ideal time in the market, or signs that your competitors will not be able to address the threat you pose. You might want to seriously consider getting patents as a demonstration of your special advantage, if appropriate. A recent study showed that startups that received patents grew over 50% faster than those without patents, in large part because they attracted more venture capital.[101]

Having shown that you have a clear market and a way of winning, you now have to show that it is worth winning by demonstrating **market sizing,** sometimes called showing your total addressable market. You can calculate this two ways. The first is "top-down," in which you work with analyst reports and other data to derive a market size. For a new premium makeup startup aimed at people with dry skin, you may start by showing how much people spend on premium makeup from market research reports and demonstrating what percentage of them have dry skin (perhaps conducting your own survey) to arrive at a market size. This is not an accurate method, of course, but when I have interviewed venture capitalists about this slide, they expect it to show several things. First, they do want to know that the market is roughly large enough, which tends to be a potential market size of around $1 billion—an admittedly arbitrary number, but one I have heard several times. Second, VCs want to know that you are thinking about the market in the right way and are focused on the right potential customers. Finally, this analysis shows that you have the ability to make a persuasive case for your startup. If you want to convince people you can make money, however, a bottom-up approach may work better.

This approach uses the unit-level economics of a particular customer to show how you will make money. How much does it cost to acquire a customer? How much profit do you make off each unit you sell? What is the turnover or churn in your market? You can use this information to figure out the customer's lifetime value after paying for all the expenses required, and if this number is positive, you are in very good shape! If you have traction, you can use the real data you are getting from customers to make an even stronger case. This is often paired with your **go-to-market** slide, where you outline how you will acquire future customers, ideally using the market sizing data just discussed.

Next, you will need to show your **competition**. The goal with your competition slide is to make sure that you can tell your audience that you actually have thought about the nature of the market you are entering. You need to convince others that the competition is not a real threat without making your audience feel like you're skipping things or being delusional. If you have a range of competitors but you fill a unique niche that nobody else does (something you have demonstrated in the magic slide), then perhaps the easiest way to compare yourself to the competition is a chart or graph. If you have real competition, though, you're going to have to address this directly because that's a question that you will certainly get from the audience. You may want to think more deeply about your key competitors and highlight your competitive advantage and strategy relative to those competitors. No matter what you do, your goal here is to show the competitive landscape, indicating to people who know the market that you have thought about this issue and that you know how to address it.

Next is the **team** slide. This is the nonfinancial slide on which VCs spend the most time.[102] The team is listed by VCs as the single most important factor in investment decisions, and VCs are particularly eager to understand more about your ability and experience.[103] An important aspect of this slide, then, is to make sure you are showing off any appropriate industry background that you have. The perceived ability of your team may depend less on what you say on this slide, however, than in the way you choose to present yourself throughout the pitch.[104] And, if your team is amazing, you may want to move the team slide further up in the presentation, as it can be a key reason you win.

You will conclude with **financial projections** and **milestones**, which will both address your present and future financials—or give the investors a breakdown of where you are and where you're going. The number of slides you'll need to indicate your current status and your financial projections will again depend a lot on your business. If it is a relatively simple straightforward app that you're selling or advertising, this can be accomplished in one slide. If it is a complex medical device for which you need FDA approval, there might be multiple slides involved showing your progress toward achieving your goal. But whatever the case, you'll want to show some financial projections and give an indication of why you think the finances of the company will operate in the way you're projecting. You will likely then have a slide with milestones, showing what you've accomplished so far and what you're planning on accomplishing in the near future.

You want to end by telling audience members what you want them to do next. Do you want to raise money? Do you want them to buy your product? Do you want them to pass on referrals to you? No matter what it is, a call to action leaves people with a clear indication of what you hope they can get out of the presentation. At this point, it's important to wrap up with the same sort of elevator pitch you started with, to clarify what you're doing and why, your audience having gained an understanding of what your product does and why it's so exciting. You can find examples of pitch decks incorporating all these elements at *www.unicorns-shadow.com*, but remember that even though you will spend an immense amount of time creating these slides, they will not get you investment on their own. The average investor spends less than four minutes looking at these slides. But they are the start of the process, not the end![105]

More than Words: Nonverbal Aspects of Pitching

Successful pitching depends on more than the words you say. The pitching process begins before you speak—with your company name. Founders often agonize over what to name their company, and, in this case, they are right to be concerned. Recent findings have suggested that the name of a company really does have an effect on its long-term success. For example, which is the luxury brand: Vipsy or Volaza? Izari or Trabe? A paper examining the naming of brands found that in both the United States and India, names were associated with luxury brands if they ended with vowel sounds, had stressed vowels and multiple syllables, and sounded foreign. So, it is not surprising that the words associated with luxury were Volaza and Izari.[106]

Even if you aren't a luxury startup, you need to consider your company name, starting with its length. Studies have shown that companies with short names are 50% more likely to grow than those with long names,[107] mirroring the best practices for picking URLs for websites, which also tend to reward short names. Research by Professors Karan Girotra and Karl Ulrich shows that the sweet spot for a domain name is seven characters long, with a 2% drop in traffic for every letter past seven in the web address.[108] This rule shouldn't restrain your naming too much, however, since you can come up with clever domain names that don't match your company name, like VC Andreessen Horowitz, which uses a16z.com instead of its long and difficult-to-spell name. You might also want to consider naming your company after yourself. Eponymous companies outperform others, especially if your name is unusual or memorable.[109]

But the self-naming trick only works for small businesses. For high-technology or high-growth startups, self-naming is associated with much slower growth. Highly innovative companies should instead pay attention to their logos. Simple logos are a good design, but they are often bad for getting investments. One study exposed investors to either slick simple logos or more cluttered logos with lots of colors and artwork. Interestingly, the investors were convinced that products associated with the complex logos were more advanced. Yet 88% of founders surveyed would have selected the simple logos because they look nicer.[110]

Research by Professors Christoph Zott and Quy Nguyen Huy has shown that successful founders go further and engage in what's called symbolic management.[111] As we noted in the previous chapter, it is hard for investors to identify which startup will succeed; investors look for signs of a startup that is going to be successful, like having the right format for a pitch deck or the right credentials. Successful founders actively manipulate symbols in a way that makes them seem to be what people expect from a founder. In fact, the biggest startup scam was largely successful because of symbolic management. Elizabeth Holmes, the founder of the now-defunct Theranos, went to extreme lengths to show personal capability through symbols: black turtlenecks in the style of Steve Jobs, the affected voice and demeanor, the Stanford drop-out résumé, and lab coats in pictures (without having lab experience). This all worked to convince others that she was the real deal. Her high-end board included former secretary of state Henry Kissinger and former defense secretary James Mattis (neither of whom knew anything about medical devices). Beautifully designed but nonfunctional blood-testing machines and showpiece office spaces further covered for substance. Holmes ultimately used all four categories of symbolic management that Zott and Huy identified.

The first category is personal—showing the world that you are a capable Founder, with a capital F. When Zuckerberg testifies in front of Congress, he wears a suit; when Zuckerberg speaks in front of his employees, he wears his famous hoodie or a T-shirt. That's an example of personal symbols: The T-shirt or hoodie is a sign that says, "I'm a successful founder"; the suit says, "I'm a successful business person in front of Congress." Showing logos of previous companies and educational institutions in your pitch deck demonstrates personal capability. Another common form of symbolic action is when founders showcase that they have given up a lot of salary to join a startup. Even in well-funded startups, founders seem to take less money than they would if they were running a different organization. Are they doing it to save money for the company? In some cases, yes. But in other cases in which founders have raised a lot of capital, their salaries don't make a material impact on the success of their companies, but they still pass on the cash. That's a form of symbolic action to indicate to your investors that you are fully committed.

Another use of symbols is based on space. Entrepreneurs need offices that look the way startup offices are expected to look when investors visit. If you are launching a startup company, that might be a burnt-out coding house in Santa Clara (straight out of HBO's *Silicon Valley*). If you're running a biomedical company, you will need something that looks like a medical lab, even if most of your work is programming. And, of course, when you have investors coming by, you might want to make that lab look more, well, like a lab, making sure that everyone is wearing white lab coats and liberally using pipettes. The idea that spaces meet expectations is another form of symbolic action in which entrepreneurs engage.

Entrepreneurs can also think about showing achievement symbolically. Getting outside recognition helps. The Forbes "30 Under 30" list can help validate that you are indeed a successful founder. But you can also demonstrate working prototypes, display awards your products have won at tradeshows, and show that you have been accepted to highly accredited accelerators. Finally, successful entrepreneurs show ties to successful stakeholders. Having prestigious advisers, mentors, and users all work as social proof of your success.

In the next chapter, we'll look at scaling up your company and how best to grow it.

The Founder's Checklist: Things to Remember

- You will need several kinds of pitches to appeal to different audiences. Many of these pitches have specific formats that you will be expected to follow.
- Use the power of storytelling and analogies to help people instantly connect with your ideas.
- Wherever possible, show, don't tell.
- Speak to your audience, using verbal and nonverbal cues to communicate your capability and vision.

Chapter 5

Growth
Lighting a Fire

Your startup doesn't have to grow.

That's right: Surveys of small business owners show that most companies don't grow and most small business owners don't want to grow. They want to build a stable organization that supports a certain standard of living, but they don't necessarily want to manage 1,000 employees and be on the cover of *Fortune* magazine. And it's completely fine to want to maintain a small organization with a steady income that isn't stressing you out too much. On the other hand, evidence shows that growing firms survive longer and are better able to weather changes in the economy and market. Plus, most startups with investors will want to see fast growth that leads to an eventual exit. That is why this book is generally aimed at growing startups, rather than stable small businesses.

At the same time, growth will not save you from mistakes. Many startups either grow too fast or they grow the wrong way. And when these things happen, it can be particularly agonizing to founders. They often find that even with 30 employees, they still need to be involved with every decision. They don't know how to delegate authority, and the company only operates because they're working 80 hours a week. In this case, founders ultimately become the limiting factor, strangling future growth. Instead, the best founders transform and change their companies as they grow, jettisoning the things that don't work and adding new structures and traditions as they do. They are also keenly aware of what's been coined Thiel's Law after the entrepreneur and venture capitalist Peter Thiel:[112] "A startup messed up at its foundation cannot be fixed."

The reason early days matter so much is that startups go through a process of *imprinting*. Early choices constrain later ones, as in the case of role imprinting.[113] Imagine you are a founder trying to decide who you're going to hire to fill an absolutely critical role in your company: the head of human resources (HR). HR can mean many different things. This hire could handle just recruiting; they could help with vital performance-enhancing aspects of the company, like promotions and training; and they could also be a lawyer who could deal with issues of employment law. You decide to hire an excellent HR person who does everything but handle the legal issues. They turn out to be great at their job, and the company starts to grow. At some point in this scenario, you need to hire a lawyer to handle the legal aspects of the human resources job. After a while, your original HR hire decides to leave the company, and now you need to hire someone to fill that HR role. That's when you discover that you inadvertently created a role built around exactly your former employee's skill sets. Now you *can't* hire an HR person who handles the legal aspects of your company because you hired a lawyer who has been growing their own legal department, and you don't want overlapping roles in your company. You're now limited only to HR people who don't handle the legal aspects of your company. By leaving, this person has left a hole in your company that's the shape of their skill set, and this means you will have to hire people to fit that skill set. Your first choice of HR director has inadvertently committed you to organizing a company with a separate legal department. And inertia is incredibly persistent. We have evidence that companies maintain much of their initial structure, even hundreds of years after they are founded![114]

So how do you make sure your initial scaling choices are good ones?

Structure and People

A word of warning: This section may seem boring. Scholars have found great ways for startups to hire, to structure companies, and to scale culture, and, much to our continual frustration, many people ignore them because they are dull and involve careful work, rather than intuitive breakthroughs.[115] While I will do my best to amaze you with facts (and there are some good ones here!), I hope I can also convince you that taking a century-old approach to corporate structure and a careful stepwise approach to hiring are the best ways to succeed. There are no real shortcuts or tricks, but the founders that pay attention to the boring details of people and structure will succeed where others fail; a strategic focus on growing your team wisely is the most important thing you will do for long-term success.

We have a lot of evidence that shows there are profound performance differences between people in organizations, so getting the right high-performing employees early is important. The most famous of performance gaps are among programmers. There are legends in Silicon Valley of the "10x engineer"—a highly productive software engineer that is 10 times better than an average one. The actual numbers are even more startling. Repeated studies found that differences between the programmers in the top 75th percentile and those in the bottom 25th percentile can be as much as 27 times along some dimensions of programming quality.[116] There are reasons to be cautious about these numbers, since the most recent studies were conducted nearly 15 years ago, and measures of performance differences have varied widely. Additionally, programming ability is just one factor in performance; if a coder can't actually function with your team, then all the ability in the world won't help, and that person can destroy more productivity than they can add. At the same time, getting a good programmer on board versus getting a mediocre programmer can make a huge difference in the productivity of your company.

Startups tend to emphasize technical skills at the expense of middle management. This is a mistake, however, as managers can play a vital role in organizing the company and making it more successful.[117] In fact, hiring middle managers early increases the chance of launching new product innovations by 33%.[118]

For managers, performance differences can also be huge. I have conducted research looking at the video game industry, trying to understand what explains performance differences between video games.[119] Different games have different levels of revenue but they are also different from each other, varying based on the genre of the game, how much money went into developing it, what platform it is on, and more. But even after you control for these factors, large gaps remain. We typically explain the gap between games as driven by companies, like Electronic Arts or Nintendo. But companies don't make products; they are made by people.

In my research, I looked at who made the games—and specifically at two different roles within the game industry. I considered the middle managers, people who help coordinate things, help run schedules, and coordinate between a senior manager and lower-level staff within the organization. I also considered the creative role in the organization: game designers. These are the people doing creative work and coming up with creative ideas inside the organization. Using thousands of games, I was able to statistically pull apart how much of the difference in revenue between games is due to the game itself and the company that produces it; how much is due to the middle manager; and how much is due to the designer on the project. What I found was interesting: 21% of the variation in performance of games (products) was explained by the company, 22% by the middle manager, and only 7% by the designer. Even in a highly creative industry, much of game success or failure can be attributed to these middle manager roles. So you need the best hires across your organization—not just in programming roles.

You also want to consider the diversity in your hiring. There are many kinds of diversity, including the ethnic, racial, or gender diversity that we discussed in the funding chapter. But diversity also includes different backgrounds, approaches, and mindsets. Having people with diverse experience often leads to what is known as task conflict, as team members push in different directions and take different approaches to solving problems. Task conflict can be productive in teams that are well managed. In teams that are dysfunctional, task conflict can decay into relationship conflict, and people can start to dislike each other, creating a possible downside to diversity.[120] Diverse teams are much more innovative, provided that founders and managers can keep the team from falling into relationship conflict.[121] The boost in innovation from diversity can be significant, however, and startups with diverse teams are more likely to raise VC and have an initial public offering.[122] Startups often find it can be hard to hire diverse candidates, because entrepreneurial companies tend to attract similar types of people, so diversity often requires extra effort from founders.[123]

How you hire is therefore really important, but much of the process is driven by myths and imitation. Most of the processes you think amount to good hiring are definitely not. Unstructured interviews, where every interviewer just has conversations with the candidate to figure out who is a good hire, are actually worse than not interviewing at all![124] Unstructured interviews make you think you have learned something about a person, even when you haven't. Research shows that people rated interviews in which candidates gave random "yes" or "no" answers to questions as having the same quality as ones in which the answers were real. And other popular methods of testing candidate quality, like the famous puzzle questions once used by Google ("How many times a day does a clock's hands overlap?"**), also fail to work.[125] In general, there is no single easy method to identify a good candidate without careful preparation and relying on either structured interviews or objective testing featuring quizzes or tasks (or, ideally, both) to see how candidates perform.[126]

Structured interviews involve first establishing a scorecard or checklist. First, you'll go through everything you want the candidate to be able to do, and you'll write down what skills and characteristics they need. You're going to be specific—not just, "I want someone

* 22.

who's entrepreneurial," but examining what that means in the context of the job. Does that mean candidates have experience as entrepreneurs? Does that mean they've taken charge in uncertain situations? Whatever it is, that goes on your scorecard. And that's going to be something you're going to look for during the interviews. You also need to coordinate with other interviewers both to create this scorecard and to set up the actual structure you're going to use. You want to make sure people ask different questions using the same shared scorecard; this way, you have a formal approach you use across every candidate that you're interviewing. This method makes comparing candidates more of a science and less of an ad hoc "gut feel" process. If everyone improvises questions, you can't compare across one candidate and you certainly can't make data-driven decisions across multiple candidates.

Good questions to ask involve past performance. Ask candidates to walk you through a time they showed leadership under pressure (or whatever criteria you identified on your scorecard). But don't just passively listen. Make it an interactive conversation and start asking questions: Why did they have to show leadership when they were junior people? What did their bosses do? How did people react to them being leaders? You're probing to get real answers and real details. When interviewing less experienced candidates, you can ask how they would handle a hypothetical situation in the future. Again, make it part of a conversation driven by a factor on your scorecard. Once you've interviewed everybody, you can simply add up the scores on all cards and average the results, picking the highest scorer. This method turns out to be more useful in many cases than having any formal discussions of candidates.[127] Using a structured approach to interviewing may be more boring than asking brainteasers, but it is the most predictive of future performance, on par with more costly measures, like job tryouts.[128]

This approach solves the people problem, but what about structure? There are three challenges every company must solve. The first challenge is a division of labor. This can be a real problem in startups because usually the founder does everything initially, but future growth requires everyone to specialize. The second challenge is coordination and how you share knowledge and decide what needs to get done. This covers critical questions of how you implement supervision, rules and procedures, and plans and budgets. The third challenge is decision rights. Early on, the founder makes all the decisions. Later, you want other people to decide things, or you're going to have a frustrating set of conversations, as people keep coming to you for every problem they encounter.

Fortunately, we have a solution for all three of these issues: decisions rights, coordination, and division of labor. Unfortunately, it's going to look really boring because you've seen it before. In fact, it has been around since 1854: the "org chart." But as a founder, when you think about building an organization, org charts are your best friend. They incorporate issues of who does what, who coordinates with whom, and who gets to make decisions. You will need to think about these structures and put them in place early, so the organization can grow effectively. Without structure, you risk growing a strange, hybrid structure that won't help you manage, won't solve issues of division of labor, won't solve coordination concerns, and will leave you a victim of people who are myopic and make bad decisions. Taking structure and hiring seriously only seems to box you in, but in reality, it will free you to focus on the important task: growing your company.

Your Buyers, Your Hires and Suppliers, and Your Wall of Fire

Unlike established companies, startups must develop strategies based on little to no information and execute them with few resources. That creates a challenge in which founders have to balance learning and doing. Too much action without reflection, and you will likely find yourself locked into a losing path. Too much reflection without action, and you may not do anything at all. Given the massive amount of responsibilities that founders have (I have spent the last four chapters giving you lists of things to do!), it is worth focusing on three key choices of entrepreneurial strategy that Professor Kevin Boudreau identified as keys to success: creating value, delivering value, and cap-turing value.[129] Or, to rephrase in a pithier way: You need to con-sider your buyers, your hires and suppliers, and your wall of fire.

Your hires and suppliers are your company and the internal and external workers that will help you execute on your plan. We dis-cussed them in the previous section, including how to hire the best people and how to organize your venture. Once you have decided what you want to handle internally in your company via hiring, you can decide what external resources—your suppliers—you need to contract with in order to deliver value to your customers. Generally, key functions should be handled internally, with outsourcing only used for one-time or specialized functions (like public relations or website design). Startups that learn to do outsourcing well can take advantage of external suppliers even better, so consider building that skill if you think outsourcing will be an important part of your growth plan.[130]

Once you have considered hires and suppliers, it is time to turn to your buyers—your customers. There are often many potential cus-tomers for your product or service, so the challenge is finding out whom to focus on. Imagine you have invented an app that can iden-tify the emotions of a person from a video with 95% accuracy, though you expect it to be 99% accurate in a year or so. It can be used in lots of different ways: Companies may want to use it for market research, police might use it to identify security threats in crowds, and par-ents might want to use it to monitor the feelings of their children. As a founder, you may be tempted to try to do everything, but this is a recipe for disaster. Startups that expand too quickly, or lose focus on a single market, will often find their attention divided and become more likely to fail. To avoid that fate, you can use research developed by Professors Josh Gans, Scott Stern, and Jane Wu, which suggests a simple rule for picking customers: "Test two, pick one."[131]

You start this process by using what you learned from your ini-tial idea testing and research (back in Chapter 2) to understand who, precisely, might value your product and why. Based on what you have learned, create a brief use case for potential customers explaining their needs in more detail.[132] To take our example from above: Marketing companies need a way to find out whether customers really like a new product, police need to know if someone might be a potential threat, and parents need to know if their kids are happy when they aren't with them. By thinking about the intensity of these needs, and what sorts of alternatives are available for customers in each market, you can generate potential "beachhead markets." These are initial customers within a wider industry that you intend to approach first, and they generally have both the greatest need and are the most accessible for you. To continue our example in selecting beachheads: We would first approach firms that conduct small focus groups as our beachhead into the marketing space (since the focus groups are collecting data in other ways, 95% accuracy is not a problem, and the technology could be a differentiator); mall security for the policing market (malls might appreciate the ability to monitor large crowds cheaply via video, even if it isn't entirely accurate); and parents of young children who can't speak as our final beachhead (parents are always anxious about young children, and the low initial accuracy won't matter if they feel good about the product).

You then need to consider three strategic factors to determine whether these beachhead markets are going to be strategically valuable.[133] First, how much will selling into the beachhead market act as a reference to future customer segments? To continue our earlier example, mall security might be looked down upon by other security officers, and so it would be a bad reference for future sales, even if the initial mall security market is profitable. Second, you also want to consider whether you will learn from your experiences working with your beachhead market in a way that will help your company thrive as it moves forward. It may be that focus group companies are good for learning because they work with many other organizations, giving you exposure to many sorts of marketing problems that you can use to improve your technology and sales. Finally, you need to consider the coherence of the beachhead customers. If you want to seem like you are a bleeding-edge technology so you can later sell your company as the most accurate way to solve complex business problems, then perhaps the market of parents with young children will be a bad choice. An app that lets parents (hopefully) understand what their babies are feeling would not be very coherent with a company that later helped do market research for the world's largest companies.

Taking into account the use cases, coherence, learning, and reference ability for each of your beachhead customers, you should select the two that seem the most promising. Now it is time to test them, using the methods described in Chapter 1 for testing assumptions. You are looking for two kinds of "fit" that let you know you are in the right market. Product-market fit shows that you have the right product for your market; it happens when you have demonstrated demand for your product and have enthusiastic customers in a market that you want to be in.[134] While there is no single measure, a good sign of product-market fit is that customers are coming to you to buy your product, rather than you having to go to them. Strategy-model fit is also important, and occurs when you find a marketing approach to these buyers that matches with the way you have structured your hires and suppliers.[135] If you have enthusiastic customers but can't develop a method of delivering products to them in a way that will eventually be profitable and meets your goals, then you don't have strategy-model fit. Whichever buyers give you the right fit is likely the best one to go after. Once you have picked a customer, avoid expanding to new markets too quickly, as companies that scale too fast are liable to fail, an all-too common occurrence.[136]

With buyers, suppliers, and hires taken care of, what about your wall of fire? Companies need a way of defending themselves against competition, as we saw in the "magic" slide in Chapter 4. Large companies have a variety of defenses from their positions in the market, including their size, the fact that they have been around longer, and, in some cases, their agility.[137] These are not usually available to entrepreneurs, who instead need to build their own wall of fire to keep competitors out without the advantage of being an incumbent. The classic test to see if you have a sustainable advantage is to use the **VRIO** model.[138]

To have a wall of fire, you must first have something **Valuable**, which is something that you can use to mitigate a threat or exploit an opportunity other companies cannot. Usually, this is something about your product that either allows you to charge more for it (you have developed a printer that needs less ink) or that you can undercut your rival's prices (you have developed a cheaper way to make printer ink). Next, your advantage must be **Rare**, so that not everyone has it, and **Inimitable**, which means that it is hard for other people to get. You can do this in a number of ways, including with intellectual property protection (you have a patent on your new ink), unusual skills (you have the only people in the world who know how to use this ink technology working with you), exclusive relationships (you have a deal with the company that makes the chemical needed for the ink), or other methods (you are a Kardashian). Finally, it must be **Organization** specific, so that you have built your company to take advantage of this resource in a way nobody else has. For example, you have built a direct-to-consumer brand around selling your ink and have made your organization flexible and fast at addressing this specialized market. If you have something giving you an advantage that passes the VRIO test, you have a wall of fire that can keep competitors away.

Building Something Good

All organizations involve building a culture, which encompasses everything from the taken-for-granted beliefs that everyone in your organization shares and the company's goals to little rituals, like company parties, that organizations often have.[139] Culture is what binds employees together and lets them understand their goals and their ways of accomplishing those goals. It is reinforced at many levels.

Uber's winning-at-all-costs culture meant that employees were always looking to find a way to be a top performer, even if that meant pushing the law to its limit. It helped rocket the company to early success but also created an environment in which legal and ethical issues were disregarded if they were done by top employees, and winning became an end in itself.[140] Uber had formal corporate values that laid out its hard-charging culture ("Always be hustlin'" was one memorable example). Uber culture was not created with public statements but rather over many individual decisions like who to hire (in the words of Arianna Huffington, "brilliant jerks"), who to reward, and what to praise or punish inside the company.[141] At the heart of Uber's culture was its founder, Travis Kalanick, who made these initial decisions and then reinforced them through both his private actions and the company's public statements (giant alcohol-fueled parties featuring Beyoncé). As the company grew, Uber's culture increasingly became a liability, leading to the exit of Kalanick and multiple lawsuits by former employees, drivers, and governments.

The culture that a founder creates is one of the most durable aspects of the company, outlasting the founder itself and carrying on the tradition of the firm. In some cases, this is quite literal. When a partner in the two-centuries-old law firm Cravath, Swaine & Moore dies, they are honored with the Cravath Walk: The living partners, clad in dark suits and white shirts, march two-by-two to the coffin, the tradition announcing, in the words of author James Stewart, "A partner has died, the firm lives."[142] Culture's long-lasting nature, in this case over hundreds of years, is a potentially huge legacy.

As a founder, you have the opportunity to shape culture to be good for your business, but also good for the world and for your employees. Research shows that unless you actively plan otherwise, much of your company's culture will be inherited, echoing the systems used by your prior employer.[143] The best founders, however, often actively shape the culture of their company, and not just by actively designing company systems and procedures. They realize that the other people in the company look to them as role models, and the way they choose to act will become a model for the company culture to emulate.[144]

As a founder, you don't have to follow the hypercompetitive cultural model of unicorns like Netflix or Uber. In fact, the belief competitive cultures are most likely to be successful turns out to be a myth—the final one that we will cover in this book. Of course, this model can work: A Stanford research project examining hundreds of startups showed that hiring top performers and building an achievement-oriented culture is indeed an approach likely to result in long-term growth.[145] However, even more successful were companies that put effort into making all employees feel like part of a family, including hiring for fit and spending lots of time developing culture. These companies found higher levels of loyalty and were more likely to survive than other startups. In fact, building organizations that encourage warmth, compassion, and understanding increases employee satisfaction and work quality.[146] And building a warm and caring company does not need to come at the expense of other factors, like accountability and agility. A recent study has shown that it is absolutely possible for a company to be good at *all* positive aspects of culture—and, indeed, the best organizations have positive cultures across many categories.[147] You can do good by being good: Creating a culture of which people want to be part is usually synonymous with creating a culture that will help your business succeed.

The Founder's Checklist: Things to Remember

- Quick growth is not always the right move.
- Remember your hires, suppliers, buyers, and wall of fire.
- For hires and suppliers: Deliberate approaches to organizing and hiring are critical to long-term success.
- For buyers: Select your customers to match your strategy, and test to see if they are the right ones.
- For your wall of fire: Make sure you have a clear sense of your long-term competitive advantage using the VRIO test.
- The best founders make decisions about the culture they want to create and shape it through human-resources approaches and role modeling.

Conclusion
Myths and Monomyths in the Shadow of the Unicorn

The advice in this book is the best evidence we have on how to be a successful founder. But I am afraid that it isn't enough. And it isn't just because founding is hard. Even if you followed all the advice in this book, it would still only take you partway toward success: There is much we still don't know about how to launch a successful startup, and the value of the advice in the book will vary in usefulness depending on circumstance. And it also isn't just because, despite my best efforts to accurately cover this diverse academic field, I certainly missed some vital nuances in the papers that I cite. Those concerns are real, but they aren't the only reason to worry about the limitations of myth busting. Systems with monomyths reward those who fit into them. We know what a hero looks like, and we assume we know what the founder of a unicorn looks like.

That is why Elizabeth Holmes was so successful in the Theranos scam. As we saw in Chapter 4, she looked the part of the founder, taking advantage of symbols like her Stanford drop-out status and her black turtleneck sweaters to convince everyone she was part of the monomyth. Her temporary success was due to her taking advantage of a script other people had written and reinforced long ago. The long shadows of Mark Zuckerberg's success, Steve Jobs's success, and Bill Gates's success linger over us today in dangerous ways.

If you don't fit the monomyth, you are likely to be penalized, even if you are right. Female founders, older founders, solo founders, and others may be statistically more successful, but if venture capitalists who have bought into the monomyth discount these founders, they won't be funded. And the fact that they weren't funded will be held against future female, older, or solo founders, and there will be fewer role models for them to emulate. It becomes a vicious cycle that reinforces the myths and darkens the shadow cast by past unicorns.

In the short term, the best way to beat the myths is to be aware of them and play into them where possible. Use the tools in the book, and the tools you will learn as a founder, to match the expectations of the monomyth where you can, while pushing the boundaries in areas that matter to you. Where you can, seek out allies: the funders and partners who realize that the greater good, and the greater profit, comes from finding people who break the mold, rather than fitting it.

But in the long term, it is even more important that we free ourselves from the entrepreneurial monomyth. Entrepreneurship is too important, both for society and for the individuals who start companies, for us to continue to chase the shadows of unicorns. Only by putting to rest the false narrative that entrepreneurship is only for the privileged few can we ensure we democratize entrepreneurship. As startups are the primary source of job creation and innovation, we need more founders, not less. Talent is everywhere; opportunity is not. By pushing back on the myths, we can start to change that.

For additional information, as well as for practical tools, files, and links, I encourage you to check out the book's website at *www.unicorns-shadow.com.*

Notes

1 Sylvia Beyer, "Gender Differences in the Accuracy of Self-Evaluations of Performance," *Journal of Personality and Social Psychology* 59, no. 5 (1990): 960.

2 Nathaniel Rich, "Silicon Valley's Start-Up Machine," *New York Times*, May 2, 2013, https://www.nytimes.com/2013/05/05/magazine/y-combinator-silicon -valleys-start-up-machine.html (accessed January 27, 2020).

3 Pierre Azoulay, Christian Fons-Rosen, and Joshua Graff Zivin, "Does Science Advance One Funeral at a Time?" No. 21788, NBER Working Papers, National Bureau of Economic Research, 2015.

4 Amanda J. Williamson, Martina Battisti, Michael Leatherbee, and J. Jeffrey Gish Williamson, "Rest, Zest, and My Innovative Best: Sleep and Mood as Drivers of Entrepreneurs' Innovative Behavior," *Entrepreneurship Theory and Practice* 43, no. 3 (2019): 582–610.

5 Matthew Wilson, "The 10 Key Personality Traits According to Top Billionaire Investors," GRG Collective, https://www.grgcollective.com/grow-your-business /private-equity-traits (accessed January 27, 2020).

6 Sari Pekkala Kerr, William R. Kerr, and Tina Xu, "Personality Traits of Entrepreneurs: A Review of Recent Literature," *Foundations and Trends in Entrepreneurship* 14, no. 3 (2018): 279–356.

7 Paul Graham, "The 18 Mistakes That Kill Startups," 2006, https://www .paulgraham.com/startupmistakes (accessed January 27, 2020).

8 Will Smale, "How Two Strangers Set Up Dropbox and Made Billions," BBC News, July 16, 2018, https://www.bbc.com/news/business-44766487 (accessed January 27, 2020).

9 Edward B. Roberts, *Entrepreneurship in High Technology: Lessons from MIT and Beyond* (New York: Oxford University Press, 1991).

10 Michael Gorman and William A. Sahlman, "What Do Venture Capitalists Do?" *Journal of Business Venturing* 4, no. 4 (1989): 231–248.

11 Joonkyu Choi, Nathan Goldschlag, John Haltiwanger, and J. Daniel Kim, "Founding Teams and Startup Performance," Working Papers 19–32, Center for Economic Studies, US Census Bureau, 2019.

12 For a thorough discussion of the issues around founding team members, see Noam T. Wasserman, *The Founder's Dilemmas: Anticipating and Avoiding the*

Pitfalls That Can Sink a Startup (Princeton, NJ: Princeton University Press, 2012).

13 Nicola Breugst, Holger Patzelt, and Philipp Rathgeber, "How Should We Divide the Pie? Equity Distribution and Its Impact on Entrepreneurial Teams," *Journal of Business Venturing* 30, no. 1 (2015): 66–94.

14 Thomas Hellmann and Noam Wasserman, "The First Deal: The Division of Founder Equity in New Ventures," No. w16922. National Bureau of Economic Research, 2011.

15 Joseph Luft and Harrington Ingham, "The Johari Window," *Human Relations Training News* 5, no.1 (1961): 6–7.

16 Evgeny Kagan, Stephen Leider, and William Lovejoy, "Equity Contracts and Incentive Design in Start-Up Teams," *Management Science* (November 2019). 10.1287/mnsc.2019.3439.

17 Eva Weinberger, Dominika Wach, Ute Stephan, and Jürgen Wegge, "Having a Creative Day: Understanding Entrepreneurs' Daily Idea Generation Through a Recovery Lens," *Journal of Business Venturing* 33, no. 1 (2018): 1–19.

18 J. Jeffrey Gish and Christopher M. Barnes, "Entrepreneurs Who Sleep More Are Better at Spotting Good Ideas," *Harvard Business Review*, October 2, 2019.

19 Denise J. Cai, Sarnoff A. Mednick, Elizabeth M. Harrison, Jennifer C. Kanady, and Sara C. Mednick, "REM, Not Incubation, Improves Creativity by Priming Associative Networks," *Proceedings of the National Academy of Sciences* 106, no. 25 (2009): 10130–10134.

20 Tom M. McLellan, John A. Caldwell, and Harris R. Lieberman, "A Review of Caffeine's Effects on Cognitive, Physical and Occupational Performance," *Neuroscience & Biobehavioral Reviews* 71 (December 2016): 294–312.

21 Paul Paulus, Jubilee Dickson, Runa Korde, Ravit Cohen-Meitar, and Abraham Carmeli, "Getting the Most out of Brainstorming Groups," in *Open Innovation: Academic and Practical Perspectives on the Journey from Idea to Market*, ed. Arthur B. Markman (Oxford University Press, 2016), 43–69.

22 Alison Beard, "Drunk People Are Better at Creative Problem Solving," *Harvard Business Review*, May–June 2018.

23 Andrew F. Jarosz, Gregory J. H. Colflesh, and Jennifer Wiley, "Uncorking the Muse: Alcohol Intoxication Facilitates Creative Problem Solving," *Consciousness and Cognition* 21, no. 1 (2012): 487–493.

24 Zhe Li, Massimo Massa, Nianhang Xu, and Hong Zhang, "The Impact of Sin Culture: Evidence from Earning Management and Alcohol Consumption in China," CEPR Discussion Papers 11475, 2016.

25 Elizabeth G. Pontikes and William P. Barnett, "The Non-Consensus Entrepreneur: Organizational Responses to Vital Events," *Administrative Science Quarterly* 62, no. 1 (2017): 140–178.

26   Saras D. Sarasvathy, "What Makes Entrepreneurs Entrepreneurial?" Darden Case No. UVA-ENT-0065, 2018.

27   Barry Nalebuff and Ian Ayres, *Why Not? How to Use Everyday Ingenuity to Solve Problems Big and Small* (Cambridge, MA: Harvard Business Review Press, 2006).

28   C. Page Moreau and Darren Dahl, "Constraints and Consumer Creativity," in *Tools for Innovation: The Science Behind the Practical Methods That Drive New Ideas*, ed. Arthur B. Markman and Kristin L. Wood (Oxford University Press, 2009), 104.

29   Massimo Garbuio, Andy Dong, Nidthida Lin, Ted Tschang, and Dan Lovallo, "Demystifying the Genius of Entrepreneurship: How Design Cognition Can Help Create the Next Generation of Entrepreneurs," *Academy of Management Learning & Education* 17, no. 1 (2018): 41–61.

30   Shelly L. Gable, Elizabeth A. Hopper, and Jonathan W. Schooler, "When the Muses Strike: Creative Ideas of Physicists and Writers Routinely Occur During Mind Wandering," *Psychological Science* 30, no. 3 (2019): 396–404.

31   Salvatore Parise, Eoin Whelan, and Steve Todd, "How Twitter Users Can Generate Better Ideas," *MIT Sloan Management Review* 56, no. 4 (2015): 21.

32   Sharique Hasan and Rembrand Koning, "Conversations and Idea Generation: Evidence from a Field Experiment," *Research Policy* 48, no. 9 (2019): 103811.

33   Alfonso Gambardella, Arnaldo Camuffo, Alessandro Cordova, and Chiara Spina, "A Scientific Approach to Entrepreneurial Decision Making: Evidence from a Randomized Control Trial," *Management Science* (forthcoming).

34   Steve Blank, "Why the Lean Start Start-Up Changes Everything," *Harvard Business Review*, May 2013.

35   Teppo Felin, Alfonso Gambardella, Scott Stern, and Todd Zenger, "Lean Startup and the Business Model: Experimentation Revisited," *Long Range Planning* (June 2019).

36   I would suggest reading Stern, Schramm, and Frick's *Harvard Business Review* essay "Do Entrepreneurs Need a Strategy?" as a starting point for some potential refinements, https://store.hbr.org/product/do-entrepreneurs-need-a-strategy /R1803B (accessed January 27, 2020).

37   Jan Brinckmann, Dietmar Grichnik, and Diana Kapsac, "Should Entrepreneurs Plan or Just Storm the Castle? A Meta-Analysis on Contextual Factors Impacting the Business Planning–Performance Relationship in Small Firms," *Journal of Business Venturing* 25, no. 1 (2010): 24–40.

38   Common approaches include the Model Canvas, which requires founders to fill in nine boxes covering topics like "Value Propositions" and "Customer Segments"; Discovery Driven Plans; and financial models built in Excel.

39   Thomas R. Eisenmann, "Business Model Analysis for Entrepreneurs," Harvard Business School Background Note 812-096, December 2011.

40 Jacqueline Kirtley and Siobhan O'Mahony, "What Is a Pivot? Explaining When and How Entrepreneurial Firms Decide to Make Strategic Change and Pivot," *Strategic Management Journal* (January 2020).

41 Ryan W. Angus, "Problemistic Search Distance and Entrepreneurial Performance," *Strategic Management Journal* (July 2019).

42 Baylee Smith and Angelina Viceisza, "Bite Me! ABC's Shark Tank as a Path to Entrepreneurship," *Small Business Economics* 50, no. 3 (2018): 463–479.

43 Susan Adams, "The Exclusive Inside Story of Ring: From 'Shark Tank' Reject to Amazon's Latest Acquisition," *Forbes*, February 27, 2018, https://www.forbes.com/sites/susanadams/2018/02/27/amazon-is-buying-ring-the-pioneer-of-the-video-doorbell-for-1-billion/#44e446f7706c (accessed January 27, 2020).

44 R. Mehta and M. Zhu, "Creating When You Have Less: The Impact of Resource Scarcity on Product Use Creativity," *Journal of Consumer Research* 42, no. 5 (2015): 767–782.

45 Wasserman, *Founder's Dilemmas.*

46 Samuel Lee and Petra Persson, "Financing from Family and Friends," *Review of Financial Studies* 29, no. 9 (2016): 2341–2386.

47 Laura Huang, Andy Wu, Min Ju Lee, Jiayi Bao, Marianne Hudson, and Elaine Bolle, "The American Angel," Angel Capital Association, November 2017.

48 Abe Othman, "Startup Growth and Venture Returns: What We Found When We Analyzed Thousands of VC Deals," AngelList Blog, December 11, 2019, https://angel.co/blog/venture-returns (accessed January 27, 2020).

49 Laura Huang and Jone L. Pearce, "Managing the Unknowable: The Effectiveness of Early-Stage Investor Gut Feel in Entrepreneurial Investment Decisions," *Administrative Science Quarterly* 60, no. 4 (2015): 634–670.

50 Cécile Carpentier and Jean-Marc Suret, "Angel Group Members' Decision Process and Rejection Criteria: A Longitudinal Analysis," *Journal of Business Venturing* 30, no. 6 (2015): 808–821.

51 Juanita Gonzalez-Uribe and Michael Leatherbee, "The Effects of Business Accelerators on Venture Performance: Evidence from Start-Up Chile," *Review of Financial Studies* 31, no. 4 (2018): 1566–1603.

52 Yael V. Hochberg and Daniel C. Fehder, "Accelerators and Ecosystems," *Science* 348, no. 6240 (2015): 1202–1203.

53 Benjamin L. Hallen, Christopher B. Bingham, and Susan L. Cohen, "Do Accelerators Accelerate? If So, How?" (April 2019), available at SSRN: https://ssrn.com/abstract=2719810.

54 Ian Hathaway, "Accelerated Companies at Series A," April 9, 2019, http://www.ianhathaway.org/blog/2019/4/9/accelerated-companies-at-series-a (accessed January 27, 2020).

55 Ufuk Akcigit, Emin Dinlersoz, Jeremy Greenwood, and Veronika Penciakova, "Synergising Ventures: The Impact of Venture Capital-Backed Firms on the Aggregate Economy," Vox EU (September 2019).

56 Christian Catalini, Jorge Guzman, and Scott Stern, "Hidden in Plain Sight: Venture Growth with or without Venture Capital," No. w26521. National Bureau of Economic Research, 2019.

57 Casey Newton, Twitter post, September 4, 2019, https://twitter.com /CaseyNewton/status/1169313947494707200 (accessed January 27, 2020).

58 David McKenzie and Dario Sansone, "Man vs. Machine in Predicting Successful Entrepreneurs: Evidence from a Business Plan Competition in Nigeria," World Bank, 2017.

59 Ramana Nanda, Sampsa Samila, and Olav Sorenson, "The Persistent Effect of Initial Success: Evidence from Venture Capital," No. w24887. National Bureau of Economic Research, 2018.

60 David H. Hsu, "What Do Entrepreneurs Pay for Venture Capital Affiliation?" *Journal of Finance* 59, no. 4 (2004): 1805–1844.

61 Michael Ewens, Ramana Nanda, and Matthew Rhodes-Kropf, "Cost of Experimentation and the Evolution of Venture Capital," *Journal of Financial Economics* 128, no. 3 (2018): 422–442.

62 Paul A. Gompers, William Gornall, Steven N. Kaplan, and Ilya A. Strebulaev, "How Do Venture Capitalists Make Decisions?" *Journal of Financial Economics* 135, no. 1 (2020): 169–190.

63 British Business Bank, "UK VC and Female Founders," British Business Bank, 2019, https://www.british-business-bank.co.uk/wp-content/uploads/2019/01 /UK_VC_and_Female_Founders_Report_British_Business_Bank.pdf (accessed January 27, 2020).

64 Lawrence Plummer, Thomas Allison, and Brian Connelly, "Better Together? Signaling Interactions in New Venture Pursuit of Initial External Capital," *Academy of Management Journal* 59, no. 5 (2015).

65 Gompers, Gornall, Kaplan, and Strebulaev, "How Do Venture Capitalists Make Decisions?"

66 Benjamin L. Hallen and Kathleen M. Eisenhardt, "Catalyzing Strategies and Efficient Tie Formation: How Entrepreneurial Firms Obtain Investment Ties," *Academy of Management Journal* 55, no. 1 (2012): 35–70.

67 Olav Sorenson and Toby E. Stuart, "Syndication Networks and the Spatial Distribution of Venture Capital Investments," *American Journal of Sociology* 106, no. 6 (2001): 1546–1588.

68 Sofie De Prijcker, Sophie Manigart, Veroniek Collewaert, and Tom Vanacker, "Relocation to Get Venture Capital: A Resource Dependence Perspective," *Entrepreneurship Theory and Practice* 43, no. 4 (2019): 697–724.

69 Huang and Pearce, "Managing the Unknowable."

70 Jason Greenberg and Ethan Mollick, "Activist Choice Homophily and the Crowdfunding of Female Founders," *Administrative Science Quarterly* 62, no. 2 (2016): 341–374.

71 Jorge Guzman and Aleksandra Kacperczyk, "Gender Gap in Entrepreneurship," *Research Policy* 48, no. 7 (2019): 1666–1680.

72 Jason Greenberg, Venkat Kuppuswamy, and Ethan Mollick, "Hubris and Humility: Gender Differences in Serial Founding Rates," available at SSRN: https://ssrn.com /abstract=2623746; Sarah Thébaud, "Business as Plan B: Institutional Foundations of Gender Inequality in Entrepreneurship across 24 Industrialized Countries," *Administrative Science Quarterly* 60, no. 4 (2015): 671–711.

73 Greenberg and Mollick, "Activist Choice Homophily and the Crowdfunding of Female Founders."

74 Dana Kanze, Laura Huang, Mark A. Conley, and E. Tory Higgins, "We Ask Men to Win and Women Not to Lose: Closing the Gender Gap in Startup Funding," *Academy of Management Journal* 61, no. 2 (2018): 586–614.

75 Ethan Mollick, Startup Game, 2014. https://hbsp.harvard.edu/product/WH0001 -HTM-ENG (accessed March 2, 2020).

76 François Neville, Juanita Kimiyo Forrester, Jay O'Toole, and A. L. Riding, "'Why Even Bother Trying?' Examining Discouragement among Racial-Minority Entrepreneurs," *Journal of Management Studies* 55, no. 3 (2018): 424–456.

77 Rembrand Koning, Sampsa Samila, and John-Paul Ferguson, "Female Inventors and Inventions" (June 2019), available at SSRN: https://ssrn.com/abstract=3401889.

78 Karl E. Weick, Kathleen M. Sutcliffe, and David Obstfeld, "Organizing and the Process of Sensemaking," *Organization Science* 16, no. 4 (2005).

79 Scott Shane, Will Drover, David Clingingsmith, and Moran Cerf, "Founder Passion, Neural Engagement and Informal Investor Interest in Startup Pitches: An fMRI Study," *Journal of Business Venturing* (August 2019).

80 David Clingingsmith and Scott Shane, "Training Aspiring Entrepreneurs to Pitch Experienced Investors: Evidence from a Field Experiment in the United States," *Management Science* 64, no. 11 (2017): 5164–5179.

81 Doug Engelbart, 1968 Demo. Transcript available at: https://www.dougengelbart .org (accessed January 27, 2020).

82 Xiao-Ping Chen, Xin Yao, and Suresh Kotha, "Entrepreneur Passion and Preparedness in Business Plan Presentations: A Persuasion Analysis of Venture Capitalists' Funding Decisions," *Academy of Management Journal* 52, no. 1 (2009): 199–214.

83 Melanie Milovac and Jeffrey Sanchez-Burks, "Positivity Makes for Poor Pitches: Affective Tone Conveyed by Entrepreneurs Shapes Support for Creative Ideas," *Academy of Management Proceedings* 2014, no. 1 (2017): 13086.

84 Jeffrey M. Pollack, Matthew Rutherford, and Brian G. Nagy, "Preparedness and Cognitive Legitimacy as Antecedents of New Venture Funding in Televised Business Pitches," *Entrepreneurship Theory and Practice* 36, no. 5 (2012): 915–939.

85 Blakley C. Davis, Keith M. Hmieleski, Justin W. Webb, and Joseph E. Coombs, "Funders' Positive Affective Reactions to Entrepreneurs' Crowdfunding Pitches: The Influence of Perceived Product Creativity and Entrepreneurial Passion," *Journal of Business Venturing* 32, no. 1 (2017): 90–106.

86 R. van Werven, O. Bouwmeester, and J. P. Cornelissen, "The Power of Arguments: How Entrepreneurs Convince Stakeholders of the Legitimate Distinctiveness of Their Ventures," *Journal of Business Venturing* 30, no. 4 (2015): 616–631.

87 Chad Navis and Mary Ann Glynn, "How New Market Categories Emerge: Temporal Dynamics of Legitimacy, Identity, and Entrepreneurship in Satellite Radio, 1990–2005," *Administrative Science Quarterly* 55 no. 3 (2010): 439–471.

88 Pollack, Rutherford, and Nagy, "Preparedness and Cognitive Legitimacy as Antecedents of New Venture Funding in Televised Business Pitches."

89 Van Werven, Bouwmeester, and Cornelissen, "The Power of Arguments."

90 Christophe Abensour, "Jaws in Space," Abensour and Partners, http://www.abensourandpartners.com/jaws-in-space/ (accessed January 27, 2020).

91 Ezra W. Zuckerman, "The Categorical Imperative: Securities Analysts and the Illegitimacy Discount," *American Journal of Sociology* 104, no. 5 (1999): 1398–1438.

92 Kimberly Chin, "Kodak Jumps over 70% a Day after Jumping on the Blockchain Bandwagon," Markets Insider, January 10, 2018, https://markets.businessinsider.com/news/stocks/kodak-stock-price-jumps-after-announcing-new-cryptocurrency-2018-1-1012816553 (accessed January 27, 2020).

93 Bram Kuijken, Gerda Gemser, and Nachoem M. Wijnberg, "Categorization and Willingness to Pay for New Products: The Role of Category Cues as Value Anchors," *Journal of Product Innovation Management* 34, no. 6 (2017): 757–771.

94 Timo van Balen, Murat Tarakci, and Ashish Sood, "Do Disruptive Visions Pay Off? The Impact of Disruptive Entrepreneurial Visions on Venture Funding," *Journal of Management Studies* 56, no. 2 (2019): 303–342.

95 Tim Phillips, *Fit to Bust: How Great Companies Fail* (Philadelphia, PA: Kogan Page, 2011).

96 David Kirsch, Brent Goldfarb, and Azi Gera, "Form or Substance: The Role of Business Plans in Venture Capital Decision Making," *Strategic Management Journal* 30, no. 5 (2009): 487–515.

97 DocSend, "What We Learned from 200 Startups Who Raised $360M," DocSend, June 16, 2015, https://docsend.com/view/p8jxsqr (accessed January 27, 2020).

98   Martin L. Martens, Jennifer E. Jennings, and P. Devereaux Jennings, "Do the Stories They Tell Get Them the Money They Need? The Role of Entrepreneurial Narratives in Resource Acquisition," *Academy of Management Journal* 50, no. 5 (2007): 1107–1132.

99   Ellen O'Connor, "Storied Business: Typology, Intertextuality, and Traffic in Entrepreneurial Narrative," *Journal of Business Communication* 39, no. 1 (2002): 36–54.

100 DocSend, "What We Learned from 200 Startups Who Raised $360M."

101 Joan Farre-Mensa, Deepak Hegde, and Alexander Ljungqvist, "What Is a Patent Worth? Evidence from the U.S. Patent 'Lottery,'" *Journal of Finance* (June 2019).

102 DocSend, "What We Learned from 200 Startups Who Raised $360M."

103 Gompers, Gornall, Kaplan, and Strebulaev, "How Do Venture Capitalists Make Decisions?"

104 Harvard Business Review, "How Do Venture Capitalists Really Assess a Pitch," *Harvard Business Review*, May–June 2017.

105 DocSend, "What We Learned from 200 Startups Who Raised $360M."

106 Abhishek Pathak, Gemma A. Calvert, and Elison A. C. Lim, "How the Linguistic Characteristics of a Brand Name Can Affect Its Luxury Appeal," *International Journal of Market Research* 59, no. 5 (2017): 567–600.

107 Jorge Guzman and Scott Stern, "Where Is Silicon Valley?" *Science* 347, no. 6222 (2015): 606–609.

108 Karan Girotra and Karl T. Ulrich, "Empirical Evidence for Domain Name Performance," INSEAD Working Paper No. 2012/41/TOM, 2012.

109 Sharon Belenzon, Aaron K. Chatterji, and Brendan Daley, "Eponymous Entrepreneurs," *American Economic Review* 107, no. 6 (2017): 1638–1655.

110 Ammara Mahmood, Jonathan Luffarelli, and Mudra Mukesh, "What's in a Logo? The Impact of Complex Visual Cues in Equity Crowdfunding," *Journal of Business Venturing* 34, no. 1 (2019): 41–62.

111 Christoph Zott and Quy Nguyen Huy, "How Entrepreneurs Use Symbolic Management to Acquire Resources," *Administrative Science Quarterly* 52, no. 1 (2007): 70–105.

112 Blake Masters, "Peter Thiel's CS183: Startup—Class 6 Notes Essay," Blake Masters, April 24, 2012, https://blakemasters.com/post/21742864570/peter-thiels-cs183-startup-class-6-notes-essay (accessed January 27, 2020).

113 Christine M. Beckman and M. Diane Burton, "Founding the Future: Path Dependence in the Evolution of Top Management Teams from Founding to IPO," *Organization Science* 19, no. 1 (2008): 3–24.

114 Victoria Johnson, "What Is Organizational Imprinting? Cultural Entrepreneurship in the Founding of the Paris Opera," *American Journal of Sociology* 113, no. 1 (2007): 97–127.

115 Don A. Moore, "How to Improve the Accuracy and Reduce the Cost of Personnel Selection," *California Management Review* 60, no. 1 (2017): 8–17.

116 Lutz Prechelt, "An Empirical Comparison of Seven Programming Languages," *IEEE Computer* 33, no. 10 (2000): 23–29.

117 Wesley D. Sine, Hitoshi Mitsuhashi, and David A. Kirsch, "Revisiting Burns and Stalker: Formal Structure and New Venture Performance in Emerging Economic Sectors," *Academy of Management Journal* 49, no. 1 (2006): 121–132.

118 Christoph Grimpe, Martin Murmann, and Wolfgang Sofka, "Organizational Design Choices of High-Tech Startups—How Middle Management Drives Innovation Performance," *Strategic Entrepreneurship Journal* 13, no. 3 (2019): 359–378.

119 Ethan Mollick, "People and Process, Suits and Innovators: The Role of Individuals in Firm Performance," *Strategic Management Journal* 33, no. 9 (2012): 1001–1015.

120 Nicola Breugst and Dean A. Shepherd, "If You Fight with Me, I'll Get Mad! A Social Model of Entrepreneurial Affect," *Entrepreneurship Theory and Practice* 41, no. 3 (2017): 379–418.

121 Alva Taylor and Henrich R. Greve, "Superman or the Fantastic Four? Knowledge Combination and Experience in Innovative Teams," *Academy of Management Journal* 49, no. 4 (2006): 723–740.

122 Christine M. Beckman, M. Diane Burton, and Charles O'Reilly, "Early Teams: The Impact of Team Demography on VC Financing and Going Public," *Journal of Business Venturing* 22, no. 2 (2007): 147–173.

123 Santiago Campero Molina and Aleksandra Kacperczyk, "Like Attracts Like? Revisiting Demographic Homophily in Entrepreneurship," *Academy of Management Proceedings* 2017, no. 1 (2017): 11544.

124 Edgar E. Kausel, Satoris S. Culbertson, and Hector P. Madrid, "Overconfidence in Personnel Selection: When and Why Unstructured Interview Information Can Hurt Hiring Decisions," *Organizational Behavior and Human Decision Processes* 137 (November 2016): 27–44.

125 Adam Bryant, "In Head-Hunting, Big Data May Not Be Such a Big Deal," *New York Times*, June 19, 2013, https://www.nytimes.com/2013/06/20/business/in-head-hunting-big-data-may-not-be-such-a-big-deal.html (accessed January 27, 2020).

126 Moore, "How to Improve the Accuracy and Reduce the Cost of Personnel Selection."

127 Warren Thorngate, Robyn M. Dawes, and Margaret Foddy, *Judging Merit* (United Kingdom: Taylor & Francis, 2008).

128 Moore, "How to Improve the Accuracy and Reduce the Cost of Personnel Selection."

129 Kevin Boudreau, "Notes on Designing Your Company," Harvard Business School Strategy Unit Working Paper, 2018, 16–131.

130 Carla Bustamante, "Strategic Choices: Accelerated Startups' Outsourcing Decisions," *Journal of Business Research* 105 (December 2019): 359–369.

131 Joshua S. Gans, Scott Stern, and Jane Wu, "Foundations of Entrepreneurial Strategy," *Strategic Management Journal* 40, no. 5 (2019): 736–756.

132 Boudreau, "Notes on Designing Your Company."

133 Joshua S. Gans, Erin Scott, and Scott Stern, *Entrepreneurial Strategy* (New York: Norton, forthcoming).

134 Tren Griffin, "12 Things about Product-Market Fit," Andreessen Horowitz, February 18, 2017, https://a16z.com/2017/02/18/12-things-about-product -market-fit/ (accessed January 27, 2020).

135 Christoph Zott and Raphael H. Amit, "The Fit Between Product Market Strategy and Business Model: Implications for Firm Performance," *Strategic Management Journal* 29, no. 1 (2008): 1–26.

136 Max Marmer, Bjoern Lasse Herrmann, Ertan Dogrultan, Ron Berman, Chuck Eesley, and Steve Blank, "Startup Genome Report Extra on Premature Scaling," *Startup Genome* 10 (2011): 1–56.

137 Boudreau, "Notes on Designing Your Company."

138 Jay B. Barney, *Gaining and Sustaining Competitive Advantage* (Pearson, 2010).

139 Edgar Schein, *Organizational Culture and Leadership*, 4th ed. (San Francisco, CA: Jossey-Bass, 2010).

140 Mike Isaac, *Super Pumped: The Battle for Uber* (New York: W. W. Norton & Company, 2019).

141 Mike Issac, "Inside Uber's Aggressive, Unrestrained Workplace Culture," *New York Times*, February 22, 2017, https://www.nytimes.com/2017/02/22 /technology/uber-workplace-culture.html (accessed February 5, 2020).

142 Peter Lattman, "Law Blog Flashback: The 1992 Death of Cravath Partner David Schwartz," *Wall Street Journal*, March 7, 2006, https://blogs.wsj.com/law/2006 /03/07/law-blog-flashback-the-1992-death-of-cravath-partner-david-schwartz/ (accessed February 5, 2020).

143 Maryann P. Feldman, Serden Ozcan, and Toke Reichstein, "Falling Not Far from the Tree: Entrepreneurs and Organizational Heritage," *Organization Science* 30, no. 2 (2019): 337–360.

144 Schein, *Organizational Culture and Leadership*.

145 James N. Baron, M. Diane Burton, and Michael T. Hannan, "The Road Taken: Origins and Evolution of Employment Systems in Emerging Companies," *Industrial and Corporate Change* 5, no. 2 (1996): 239–275.

146 Sigal G. Barsade and Olivia A. O'Neill, "What's Love Got to Do with It? A Longitudinal Study of the Culture of Companionate Love and Employee and Client Outcomes in a Long-Term Care Setting," *Administrative Science Quarterly* 59, no. 4 (2014): 551–598.

147 Donald Sull, Hyo Kang, Neil C. Thompson, and Lucy Hu, "Trade-offs in Firm Culture? Nope, You Can Have It All," (August 2018), available at SSRN: https://ssrn.com/abstract=3228167 (accessed February 5, 2020).

Index

About the Author

Ethan Mollick is an associate professor at the Wharton School of the University of Pennsylvania, where he studies and teaches innovation and entrepreneurship. His papers have been published in top management journals and have won multiple awards. His work on crowdfunding is the most cited article in management published in the last five years.

Prior to his time in academia, Ethan cofounded a startup company, and he currently advises a number of startups and organizations. As the academic director and cofounder of Wharton Interactive, he works to transform entrepreneurship education using games and simulations. He has long had interest in using games for teaching, and he coauthored a book on the intersection between video games and business that was named one of the American Library Association's top 10 business books of the year. He has built numerous teaching games, which are used by tens of thousands of students around the world.

Mollick received his PhD and MBA from MIT's Sloan School of Management and his bachelor's degree from Harvard University, magna cum laude.

About Wharton School Press

Wharton School Press, the book publishing arm of the Wharton School of the University of Pennsylvania, was established to inspire bold, insightful thinking within the global business community.

Wharton School Press publishes a select list of award-winning, best-selling, and thought-leading books that offer trusted business knowledge to help leaders at all levels meet the challenges of today and the opportunities of tomorrow. Led by a spirit of innovation and experimentation, Wharton School Press leverages groundbreaking digital technologies and has pioneered a fast-reading business book format that fits readers' busy lives, allowing them to swiftly emerge with the tools and information needed to make an impact. Wharton School Press books offer guidance and inspiration on a variety of topics, including leadership, management, strategy, innovation, entrepreneurship, finance, marketing, social impact, public policy, and more.

Wharton School Press also operates an online bookstore featuring a curated selection of influential books by Wharton School faculty and Press authors published by a wide range of leading publishers.

To find books that will inspire and empower you to increase your impact and expand your personal and professional horizons, visit *wsp.wharton.upenn.edu.*

About the Wharton School

Founded in 1881 as the world's first collegiate business school, the Wharton School of the University of Pennsylvania is shaping the future of business by incubating ideas, driving insights, and creating leaders who change the world. With a faculty of more than 235 renowned professors, Wharton has 5,000 undergraduate, MBA, executive MBA, and doctoral students. Each year 18,000 professionals from around the world advance their careers through Wharton Executive Education's individual, company-customized, and online programs. More than 99,000 Wharton alumni form a powerful global network of leaders who transform business every day.

www.wharton.upenn.edu

Printed in the USA
CPSIA information can be obtained
at www.ICGtesting.com
JSHW080002150824
68134JS00021B/2233